Stumpwork
Dragonflies

Stumpwork *Dragonflies*

Jane Nicholas

First published in 2000 by

Sally Milner Publishing Pty Ltd

PO Box 2104

Bowral NSW 2576

AUSTRALIA

© Jane Nicholas 2000

Design by Ken Gilroy
Editing by Lyneve Rappell
Photography Sergio Santos
Printed in Hong Kong

*National Library of Australia
Cataloguing-in-Publication data:*
Nicholas, Jane
Stumpwork Dragonflies.

Includes index.
ISBN 1 86351 262.4

1. Stump work. 1. Title. II. Title:
Stump work dragonflies. (Series:
Milner craft series).

764.44

Endpapers: Long Cushion Cover, T.80 - 1946, c. 1600, 20" x 42".
Courtesy of the Trustees of the Victoria and Albert Museum, London.

Black velvet, long cushion cover, c.1600, ornamented with thirteen different slips including columbine, pink, marigold, rose, borage, campion, daffodil, grapes and gourds. These applied motifs, worked in silk on linen canvas, are edged with two rows of silver-gilt thread. In the spaces between are the lion and unicorn, an elephant, an owl and a parrot, a rabbit, cock, hare, dog and various strange beasts, twelve winged insects and twenty-five centipedes. Embroidered in silk, silver and silver-gilt thread in stem, satin, herringbone, tent and cross stitch, with laid and couched work.

To the memory of my father:
a meticulous craftsman
and a collector.

Contents

The burnished dragonfly is thine attendant
And tilts against the field,
And down the listed sunbeam rides resplendent
In steel blue mail and shield.

Henry Wadsworth Longfellow
1807-1882

INTRODUCTION

While all aspects of that curious form of raised embroidery, known as stumpwork, are appealing, nothing captures the imagination more than the idea of 'stumpwork insects'. These small and often exquisitely beautiful creatures, lend themselves perfectly to interpretation in threads, exotic silks and gauzes, beads and miscellaneous 'treasures'. The enthusiasm for including insects in our needlework is as evident today as it was for our predecessors.

The Elizabethan embroideress filled any available space with a most inventively treated, and fantastic array of worms, caterpillars, spiders, craneflies, butterflies and unidentifiable insects.

(Snook 1974, p. 46)

When a fellow embroiderer, with a passion for insects, suggested that I work a specimen box, the seed was sown. What started as a collection of insects in one specimen box, rapidly expanded into a collection of specific insects, grouped according to order and suborder, in a series of boxes! The inspiration for this book, and the first specimen box to be completed, is order Odonata — the dragonfly.

This beautiful water insect, with its iridescent body, fragile, gauzy wings that shimmer and gleam like jewels in the sunlight, and large eyes that look like beads, are the most elegant and lovely of the creatures that were so popular in the past. Descended from a very ancient order, the dragonfly holds a major place in world folklore and the decorative arts.

This book gives a brief historical survey of the insect—with an emphasis on the dragonfly – in sixteenth and seventeenth century needlework, and touches on the natural history and anatomy essential for stitching a realistic specimen. There are comprehensive instructions for 'How to Embroider a Stumpwork Dragonfly', the specimen box (with nine dragonflies and damselflies), and three projects.

Preparing this book has been quite a self-indulgent experience; providing for the fascination of research, the challenge of interpretation and the pleasure of stitching. Enjoy!

Natural

NATURAL HISTORY

Dragonflies and damselflies belong to an order of insects (Odonata), which goes back in the fossil record at least 200 million years. Fossils of their close ancestors, Protodonata, have been found in the coal layers of the Carboniferous Period. These huge, carnivorous, dragonfly-like insects, with a wingspan of up to 30" (75 cm), were the largest insects known on earth 300 million years ago.

*D*ragonflies occur near ponds and rivers from the tropics, where they are most numerous and varied, to the Arctic Circle. Mostly between $1^1/_8$" and $3^5/_8$" (30 and 90 mm) long, they include some huge forms exceeding 6" (150 mm), and small fragile specimens of less than $3/_4$" (20 mm).

Dragonflies are known for their bright, metallic bodies, and gauzy wings. Male dragonflies are usually more brightly coloured than females, although colour differences between the sexes are not universal. Some dragonfly colours are true pigments, others are the result of light diffraction in the body's outer layer.

> *The magical shimmer of a dragonfly's wings can only be seen while the insect is alive. The iridescence appears when sunlight strikes a thin film of liquid suspended between the layers of the wings. When the dragonfly dies, the liquid dries up and the rainbow brilliance disappears.*
>
> (Koch 1998)

They are specialised hunters, using their movable heads, sharp cutting mouthparts, large compound eyes, four independently moving wings and grasping legs to catch and eat their prey. Damselflies catch small soft-bodied insects such as mosquitoes and little moths, while the dragonfly – a far more powerful predator – will eat anything it can catch and hold.

The order Odonata comprises over 5,000 species, which can be divided into two main suborders – Anisoptera (dragonflies) and Zygoptera (damselflies). They possess the following distinguishing features.

Dragonflies

· robust bodies

· large eyes touching or very close together

· back wings are broader at the base than
  front wings

· powerful flight

· wings spread at right angles to the body when at rest

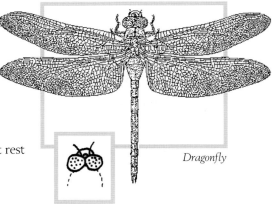

Dragonfly

Head and eyes

Damselflies

· slender, delicately built bodies

· smaller eyes, wide apart

· four narrow wings joined to thorax by very slender
  petiole

· flight is weak and fluttering

· usually fold the wings backward above the body
  when at rest

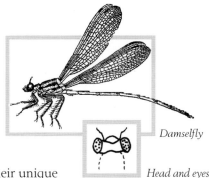

Damselfly

Head and eyes

Petiole

Dragonflies usually mate in flight in their unique
'wheel position'. Pairs are often seen flying together,
with the tip of the male abdomen gripping the neck of the female, and the female
abdomen curved round to reach the undersurface of his abdomen. Female dragonflies,
guarded by the male, lay their eggs on or inside water plants, or over the
surface of ponds or steams. The nymphs or larvae hatch from the eggs within
five to fifteen days.

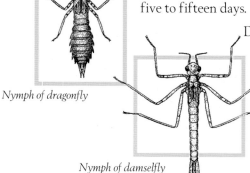

Nymph of dragonfly

Nymph of damselfly

Dragonflies have a pattern of growth and development
(incomplete or simple metamorphosis) in which the
young differ greatly from their parents. The wing-
less, aquatic nymph is shorter, broader and flatter than
the flight-oriented adult, and breathes by means of gills.
It is fiercely predatory and feeds on other insects,

12

tadpoles and small fish using a set of hinged mouthparts called a 'mask'.

The nymph remains in the water for one to five years during which time it moults (loses its skin) up to fifteen times. When the nymph is fully grown, it crawls out of the water onto a plant stem or rock, moults for the final time, and emerges as a winged adult which can fly as soon as the soft, cellophane-like wings have expanded and hardened.

Adult dragonflies live for only a few weeks or months.

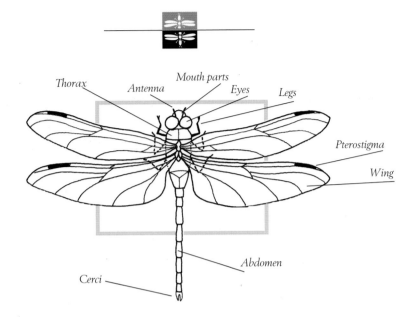

Thorax Antenna Mouth parts Eyes Legs Pterostigma Wing Abdomen Cerci

ANATOMY OF A DRAGONFLY

Abdomen

A thin, long, cylindrical abdomen of ten discernable, flexible segments, with paired cerci on segment ten.

Wings

Dragonflies have a powerful flight with speeds clocked up to 97 km/hour. Four wings move independently making them agile, highly manoeuvrable fliers. Veins and pterostigma (opaque wing markings), usually black, brown or dull yellow, are sometimes brightly coloured.

Thorax

The three-segmented thorax of dragonflies is tilted to push the three pairs of legs forward (which helps in grasping prey), and the two pairs of wings backward (keeping them clear of the legs when flying).

Head

The large head – with tiny, pointed antennae and biting mouthparts – is adapted for predation. Dragonflies have huge eyes, with strong binocular vision; damselflies achieve this with smaller eyes, by having them widely separated on a broad head.

Legs

The rather short, slender legs are covered with spines and are highly adapted for seizing and holding prey or clinging to stems, but not for walking. When flying, the legs are held forwards to form a 'basket' to capture insects.

Dragonflies are sometimes called 'horse stingers' and 'devil's darning needles', the latter from the superstition that they could sew up the eyes, ears and mouth of a sleeping child, or that if you told a lie, a dragonfly would sew up your mouth! Such a belief arose from the dragonfly's appearance – the long, thin abdomen, which, in the male, has appendages at the end that suggest the head of a large darning needle.

Insects

INSECTS AND NEEDLEWORK

The quantity and variety of insects revealed in the needlework of the sixteenth and seventeenth centuries, reflects both the scientific interest and delight that they inspired at the time. Even Queen Elizabeth's wardrobe included gowns *'glittering with flies, worms, grasshoppers and spider webs'*. (Beck 1992, p. 126)

C lothing (both men's and women's) and home furnishings (such as cushions long pillow covers, stumpwork cabinets and mirror frames) were richly embroidered with a variety of flowers, fruits, birds and animals. The otherwise empty space between motifs was filled with an extraordinary assortment of insects. Bees, flies, ladybirds, dragonflies, moths, beetles, worms, snails, grasshoppers and crickets, craneflies, caterpillars and centipedes, spider webs and spiders, butterflies and unidentifiable insects can all be found in Elizabethan and Stuart embroideries.

A wonderful example is a long pillow cover, worked on linen in pale shades of coloured silk, with the great assortment of *'10 flowers, 3 birds, 4 fishes, 1 shell, 4 beasts, 1 reptile, 4 large and 23 small insects, and 41 little beetles scattered as if sequins.'* (Snook 1974, p. 72)

Insects:
Copper engraving by
Jacob Hoefnagel from
the 1630 edition of
Georg Hoefnagel's
Archetypa.
(Dance 1989, p. 28)

17

These needleworkers did not create their own designs. They made extensive use of printed sources of all kinds, or had designs drawn out on to fabric, ready for working, by professionals who offered this service. The designs for these insects were printed and sold, by print sellers in London, in pattern books or as individual sheets of engravings.

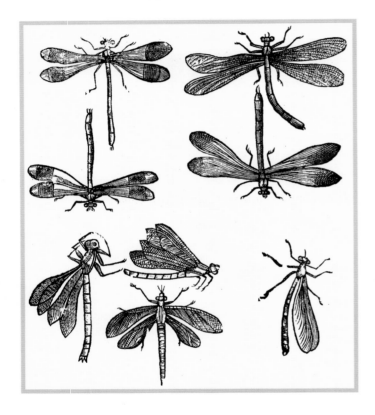

The print sellers often, and unashamedly, copied from earlier sources, such as the woodcuts or engravings that illustrated manuscripts, printed herbals and natural history works.

One of the most popular was the Archetypa of Georg Hoefnagel (1592); one of the last, and most charming, natural history books to be published in the sixteenth century. The illustrations, from the copper engravings made by his son Jacob, comprise figures of plants, animals and insects attractively assembled on each page. Jacob Hoefnagel's images of insects were minute, finely detailed, brightly illuminated and vividly coloured – qualities that invited close visual scrutiny.

Dragonflies and Damselflies: a page from Thomas Moffet's Insectorum Theatrum, *1634, illustrated with woodcuts.*

Some of the insects to be found embroidered on an early seventeenth century long cushion cover, closely resemble the illustrations in Thomas Moffet's *Theatre of Insects* (1634). A pioneering entomological work, *Insectorum Theatrum* is illustrated with woodcuts – mostly thumbnail size – which embellish the text throughout.

SEVENTEENTH CENTURY DRAGONFLIES

*O*f all the insects that were so popular in the past, the dragonfly – with its iridescent body and wing colours that glisten like jewels in the sunlight – is the most elegant and lovely. The following specimens, inspired by and drawn from, seventeenth century sources, have been worked in techniques popular at the time: blackwork, goldwork and work in coloured silk, including needlelace. Use these designs, enlarged if desired, to work your own interpretations of these beautiful creatures. The sizes of the embroidered insects varied greatly – there is an example of a dragonfly, worked on a sleeve, which appears to be about 4" (10 cm) long!

Blackwork

Blackwork is a term used to describe various kinds of embroidery worked in black silk floss on white linen. This monochrome embroidery was occasionally worked in red, green or blue silk, and was often embellished with silver or silver-gilt thread and spangles. There are two main methods of working.

Blackwork could be worked as tiny geometric patterns on a counted thread background. Worked in double running stitch, also known as Holbein stitch or Spanish stitch, this form of blackwork was frequently used to decorate fine linen collars, cuffs and ruffs.

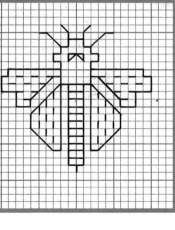

Example 1. This traditional blackwork motif is from a sixteenth century sampler. Worked in double running stitch over two threads, on 32 threads/inch Belfast linen, with one strand of black thread in a size 28 Tapestry needle.

Blackwork could be worked as a linear stitch on fine linen or cambric, using a wide variety of stitches such as back stitch, stem stitch and chain stitch. It was used to embellish outer garments such as jackets and caps, and to decorate and strengthen fine linen underclothes such as shirts, smocks and chemises.

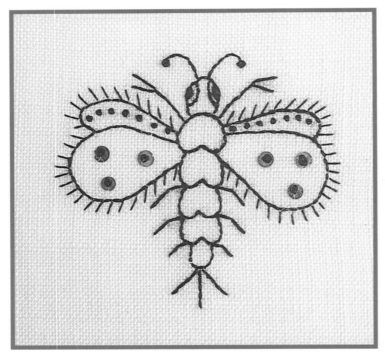

Example 2. This motif is from *A Schole-house for the Needle*, published by Richard Shorleyker in 1632; a pattern book with a range of designs which could be copied.

Worked in back stitch on fine linen with one strand of black thread in a size 10 Crewel needle, and embellished with metal spangles.

In Japan, dragonflies traditionally have been held in high regard, with warriors including dragonfly patterns on their armour as a symbol of victory

Embroidery in coloured silk

A wide variety of surface stitches (such as chain, stem, satin and herringbone stitch) and detached needlelace stitches (such as buttonhole stitch filling) were worked in coloured silk, and were seldom used without metal thread.

This dragonfly is drawn from an early seventeenth century linen long cover, embroidered in silk in long and short, stem, herringbone and satin stitches, with laid and couched work.

Example 3. Worked on grey silk with variegated stranded cotton, fine metallic thread and beads.

Wings	corded (with metallic thread) detached buttonhole stitch in variegated thread
Abdomen	padded satin stitch in variegated thread
Head and Thorax	padded satin stitch with lattice couching
Eyes	beads
Legs	straight stitches with fine metallic cord

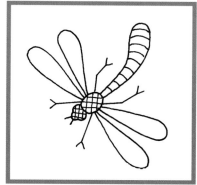

The following five dragonflies were all drawn from an Elizabethan black velvet long-cushion cover, ornamented with thirteen flower slips, birds, animals and a wonderful collection of twelve winged insects and twenty-five centipedes. Worked in silk, silver and silver-gilt thread in tent, stem, satin, herringbone and cross stitch, with laid and couched work.

Example 4. Worked on ivory satin with variegated stranded silks, chenille, iridescent couching thread, fine metallic thread and beads.

Wings	couched iridescent thread
Abdomen	puffy couching in silk
Thorax	satin stitch in chenille
Head and Eyes	beads
Legs	straight stitches in fine metallic cord

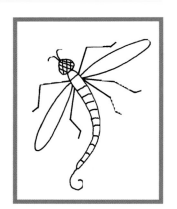

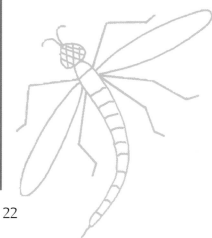

Example 5. Worked on ivory satin with gold passing thread, metallic thread and beads.

Wings	couched gold passing thread and petite beads
Abdomen	small bugle beads
Thorax	metallic braid
Head and Eyes	beads
Legs	straight stitches in fine metallic cord

 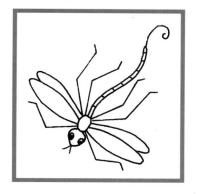

Example 6. Worked on black velvet with silver pearl purl, metallic threads and beads.

Wings	detached buttonhole stitch in silver thread
Abdomen	couched silver pearl purl
Thorax	freshwater pearl
Head and Eyes	beads
Legs	straight stitches in fine metallic cord

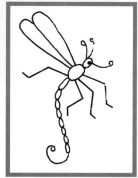

Example 7. Worked on russet velvet with gold metal purl and milliary, bronze kid, fine gold metallic thread and beads.

Wings	herringbone in fine gold thread, edged with couched gold milliary
Abdomen	couched gold purl, padded with felt
Thorax	padded bronze kid
Head and Eyes	beads
Legs	straight stitches in fine metallic cord

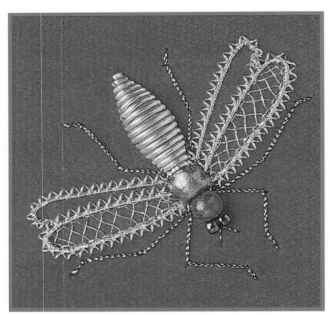

A symbol of summer for the Chinese, the dragonfly also represented instability because of its apparently haphazard flight pattern.

Example 8. Worked on ivory satin with silks, organza, fine metallic threads, chenille and beads.

Wings	outline and herringbone in fine metal thread over organza
Abdomen	satin stitch in silk thread
Thorax	satin stitch in chenille
Head and Eyes	satin stitch and beads
Legs	straight stitches in fine metallic cord

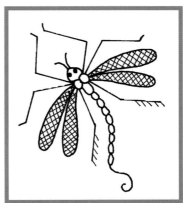

Interveniat pro Nobis quæsumus domine Jesu Christe Apud tuam Clementiam glo
riosissima on genitrix virgo semper Maria mater tua. Cuius sacratissimam mi
sericordiam in hora passionis et mortis tuæ doloris gladius pertransiuit ò, domi
ne Jesu christe pater dulcissime Rogo te ob Amorem Illius gaudij quod dilecta Mater
tua habuit quando te uidit Et ei apparuisti in illa Sanctissima nocte Pasch, et per
gaudium quod habuit quando te uidit glorificatum diuinitatis clauitate deprecor te quatenus
me illumines septem donis spiritus sancti ut tuam uoluntatem adimplere ualeam omnibus
diebus vitæ meæ. O domine Jesu Christe, adoro te in Cruce pendentem et coronam Spi
neam in capite portantem, deprecor te ut tua crux liberet me ab angelo percu
tiente. O domine Jesu Christe, adoro te in cruce uulneratum, felle et aceto potatum,
deprecor te ut tua uulnera sint remedium animæ meæ. O. domine Jesu Christe æ.

MORE DRAGONFLY DESIGN SOURCES

*T*he combination, 'insects and needlework', still holds much appeal for the current generation of embroiderers. Just as our predecessors obtained ideas for designs from printed sources of all kinds, we too have a wealth of information and inspiration available to us.

Embroidery is about looking - looking at how the effects, past and present, have been achieved, assessing them, seeing how they might be adapted to fit into one's own scheme of things.
(Beck 1997, p. 11)

It is useful, and great fun, to keep an 'ideas' diary containing sketches, pressed flowers, fabric swatches, magazine cuttings, pressed insect wings, thread samples, postcards, photographs etc., as ideas for potential projects. Then, when you are ready to commence a new work, you have the reference and inspiration at your fingertips.

The following collection of design sources, and ideas for using embroidered dragonflies, was culled from my 'ideas' diary, which I share here in the hope that they may 'get you stitching'!

Natural History Sources

Entomology and natural history books, and natural history museums and their publications are wonderful resources.

Illuminated Manuscripts

Illuminated borders in fifteenth century books of hours, often have a variety of flowers (forget-me-nots, violets, clover, chamomile), butterflies and gauzy-winged dragonflies, all perfectly true to nature, depicted on their gold or cream vellum backgrounds. These detailed illustrations make charming subjects for stumpwork embroidery.

**Blackwork
Dragonflies**

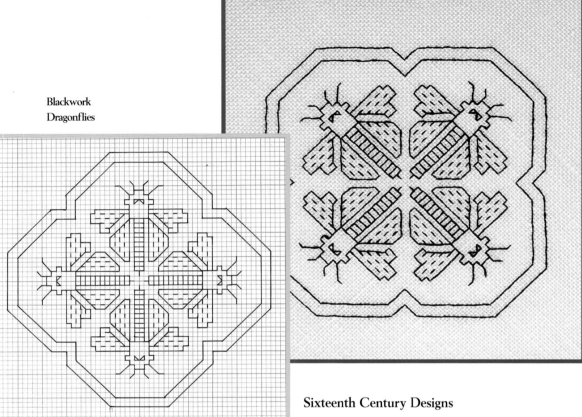

Sixteenth Century Designs

This sixteenth century blackwork dragonfly motif would look lovely embroidered on the pocket of a white linen shirt. Work over waste canvas if the linen is too fine to count.

Combine four dragonfly motifs in a geometric design, and enclosed them in a border. This project can be made into a square pincushion.

- You will need cream evenweave linen – 32 threads/inch (Belfast), black stranded cotton and a size 28 Tapestry needle. I worked this piece with a muslin backing, in a 6" embroidery hoop, but this is optional, as many people prefer to work without a hoop or a backing.
- Following the chart, work the design in double running stitch, over two threads, using one strand of black cotton.

28

Book Ornament

In the nineteenth-century, printers frequently used engraved headpieces and tailpieces to decorate the beginning or end of a book or chapter. This small, decorative tailpiece of a stylised dragonfly and flowers, made by Henri Caruchet, was the inspiration for the project 'Dragonfly and Viburnum'.

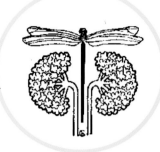

*Floral
Ornament*

Appliqué and Patchwork

A contemporary greeting card of dragonflies, worked in appliqué, was the inspiration for this notebook cover, using an enlarged dragonfly motif from the Elizabethan long cushion. Worked on a slubbed cotton background, with chenille and pearl-cotton threads and ethnic glass beads, a cotton print replaces organza for the appliquéd wings of this dragonfly. A border of pieced fabric completes this removable cover, the size of which can be adjusted to fit any small notebook or address book.

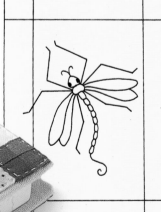

Oriental Inspiration

The Japanese family crest, with its origin in the eleventh century, is an ornamental emblem displayed on costumes on formal occasions. These circular, often symmetrical motifs, which can also fit within a square, have developed into one of the richest graphic art traditions in the world, with over 4,000 individual designs. Dragonflies, with their elegant symmetry, lend themselves perfectly to pattern making within this tradition.

Decorative Objects

Examples of the use of the dragonfly as a decorative motif can be found in a range of eras and cultures: from the drawings of dragonflies on ancient Japanese *dotaku* (bronze bell-shaped ceremonial objects) to the realistically painted dragonfly in the late eighteenth century glass button shown on page 27.

The design for this exotic dragonfly – worked with couched metal threads, appliqué and beads – was adapted from this beautiful enamelled, Art Nouveau button.

THE SPECIMEN BOX

T he sixteenth century was an age of wonder. With the discoveries of foreign lands, and the excitement of finding new things in the world, developed a passion for collecting and displaying wondrous objects in 'cabinets of curiosity'. The earliest and most basic classification was to assemble 'like' objects: 'naturalia, *such as minerals, stuffed animals, plants, ethnographic artifacts, and fossils, and* artificialia, *with a special fondness for paintings, weapons, scientific instruments, and mechanical marvels such as clocks and automata.'* (Belk 1995, p. 32)

Eventually, classifications became more detailed and more specialised cabinets emerged, with the collecting of natural history specimens (and the embroidering of insects) becoming a passion in England in the seventeenth century. The advent of the microscope in the mid-seventeenth century, led to an increased interest in insects and many discoveries about their anatomy.

The scientific study of insects, entomology, has led to the classification of insects into the class Insecta, which is divided into twenty-nine orders. Each order is further subdivided into families, genus and species (Linnaeus identified insects into genus and species in 1758).

A specimen box is a perfect way to 'collect' stumpwork insects. It provides for the fascination of research, the challenge of interpretation and the joy of stitching.

This is a specimen box of dragonflies – order Odonata. This order can be divided into two main suborders: Anisoptera, the true dragonflies, of which there are five examples, and Zygoptera, the more delicate damselflies, with four specimens.

These insects were embroidered for pleasure, often with 'treasures' from many years of collecting. For example, the abdomen of the Red Skimmer Dragonfly was worked with a scrap of orange pigskin that I have had for 25 years! Therefore, the instructions cannot include specific materials, but instead, encourage you to indulge in the search for just the right thread, fabric or bead.

If you would like to work your own specimen box of three, four or nine dragonflies, the following information may be helpful.

· The methods for working all the parts of the dragonfly can be found in the chapter, 'How to Embroider a Stumpwork Dragonfly'.

· The background fabric, a very finely textured silk, was chosen to represent parchment.

· The dragonflies are not true to scale. The wingspans and lengths are indicated in the notes.

· The diagrams are actual size and have been adapted from entomological drawings. Trace a skeleton outline and the wing shapes from these diagrams.

· The dragonflies are as 'entomologically accurate' as the limitations of materials will allow. The challenge is to interpret the various parts in fabrics, threads and beads!

· All the wings have one of their layers on the bias, and no Vliesofix has been used.

· The wires (28 gauge uncovered) are stitched with Rayon Madeira No. 40 Machine Embroidery Thread.

· Kreinik Metallic Cord is a very fine twisted metallic thread and is available in a wide range of colours, such as gold/black, perfect for insect veins and legs.

· The pterostigma is stitched with Metallic Madeira No. 40 colour 70 (black).

· The thread that I cannot be without is Kreinik Blending Filament colour 085 peacock-green.

THE DRAGONFLY SPECIMEN BOX

Variable Damselfly

Coenagrion pulchellum

Order: Odonata

Suborder: Zygoptera

Family: Coenagrionidae

Ruddy Darter

Sympetrum sanguineum

Order: Odonata

Suborder: Anisoptera

Family: Libellulidae

Broad-bodied Chaser

Libellula depressa

Order: Odonata

Suborder: Anisoptera

Family: Libellulidae

Club-tailed Dragonfly

Gomphus vulgatissimus

Order: Odonata

Suborder: Anisoptera

Family: Gomphidae

Common Hawker

Aeshna juncea

Order: Odonata

Suborder: Anisoptera

Family: Aeshnidae

Banded Demoiselle

Calopteryx splendens

Order: Odonata

Suborder: Zygoptera

Family: Calopterygidae

Blue Damselfly

Diphlebia coerulescens

Order: Odonata

Suborder: Zygoptera

Family: Amphipterygidae

Red Skimmer Dragonfly

Libellula saturata

Order: Odonata

Suborder: Anisoptera

Family: Libellulidae

Emerald Damselfly

Lestes sponsa

Order: Odonata

Suborder: Zygoptera

Family: Lestidae

To the native American Indian, the dragonfly stood for swift activity.

Variable Damselfly

Coenagrion pulchellum

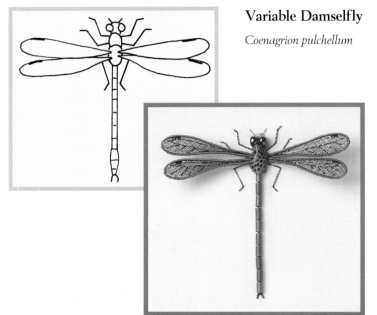

Order: Odonata

Suborder: Zygoptera

Family: Coenagrionidae

Variable Damselfly males are bright blue with an exceptionally thin, slender abdomen. The females are predominantly blue or green, with a variety of markings on their bodies. This species inhabits stagnant water. Wingspan $1\,{}^5/_8$″ (42 mm); length $1\,{}^1/_4$″ (32 mm).

Abdomen: Beaded	Small ($^1/_8$″ or 3 mm) blue/green bugle beads
	Fine green/black metallic thread
Wings: Four Detached	Aqua organza ribbon (upper layer)
	Blue/gold metallic organza (lower layer)
	Aqua rayon machine thread
	Peacock-green blending filament (veins)
	Fine black metallic thread (pterostigma)
Thorax: Padded Leather	Green emu-leg skin
Head:	Eyes, $^1/_8$″ (3 mm) dark teal beads
	Mouthparts, satin stitch in gold silk
Legs/Antennae:	Fine green/black metallic thread

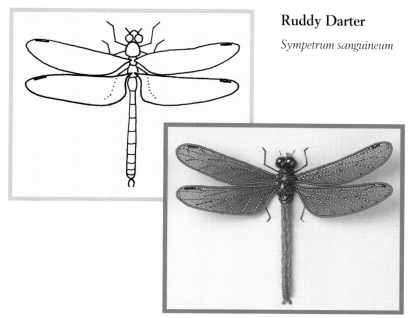

Ruddy Darter

Sympetrum sanguineum

Order: Odonata
Suborder: Anisoptera
Family: Libellulidae

Darter dragonflies have shorter, sturdier bodies. The male has a bright-red abdomen with black tail marks. The female's abdomen is russet. This species habitually spends time clinging to waterside vegetation, but is often found far away from any water. Wingspan 2 $^{1}/_{8}$″ (54 mm); length 1 $^{3}/_{8}$″ (35 mm).

Abdomen: Raised Stem Stitch Band	
	Russet stranded silk and variegated cotton
	Worked in alternate rows
Wings: Four Detached	Blue/orange organza (upper layer)
	Red/black organza (lower layer)
	Russet rayon machine thread
	Fine bronze/black metallic thread (veins)
	Fine black metallic thread (pterostigma)
Thorax: Padded Leather	Brown snake-skin
Head:	Eyes, $^{1}/_{8}$″ (3 mm) purple 'pearl' beads
	Mouthparts, satin stitch in gold silk
Legs/Antennae:	Fine brown/black metallic thread

Broad-bodied Chaser

Libellula depressa

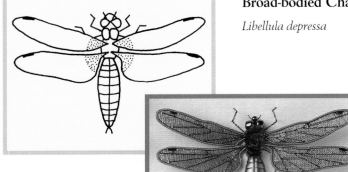

Order: Odonata

Suborder: Anisoptera

Family: Libellulidae

The Broad-bodied Chaser has a strikingly flat abdomen, in colours from blue to olive-brown. Their wings have bronze-coloured wedges at the inner corners. This species frequents small pools of stagnant water. Wingspan 3″ (76 mm); length 1 ³/₄″ (45 mm).

Abdomen: Padded Leather

Bronze kid padded with felt

Fine gold/charcoal metallic thread

Wings: Four Detached Bronze organza (upper layer)

Bronze/black metal organdie (lower layer)

Insert circles of copper metal organdie

Bronze rayon machine thread

Fine brown/black metallic thread (veins)

Fine black metallic thread (pterostigma)

Thorax: Wrapped Chenille Thread

Brown chenille thread

Head: Eyes, ¹/₈″ (3 mm) blue/black beads

Mouthparts, petite bead

Legs/Antennae: Fine gold/charcoal metallic thread

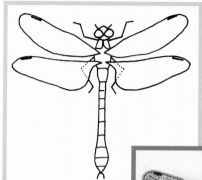

Club-tailed Dragonfly

Gomphus vulgatissimus

Order: Odonata
Suborder: Anisoptera
Family: Gomphidae

The male of this series of dragonflies has yellow markings on its brownish-black club-ended body. The female's abdomen is less waisted. It flies in the vicinity of clean streams and rivers, but also wanders quite far afield. Wingspan $2 \frac{1}{2}$ " (64 mm); length 2" (50 mm).

Abdomen: Leather Wrapped Toothpick

Brown snakeskin

Fine brown/black metallic thread

Wings: Four Detached   Green/multi-coloured organza (upper layer)

Gold mottled organza (lower layer)

Light bronze rayon machine thread

Fine variegated metallic thread (veins)

Fine black metallic thread (pterostigma)

Thorax: Wrapped Chenille Thread

Olive chenille thread

Head: Eyes, $\frac{1}{8}$" (3 mm) wine-coloured beads

Mouthparts, petite bead

Legs/Antennae: Fine wine/black metallic thread

Common Hawker

Aeshna juncea

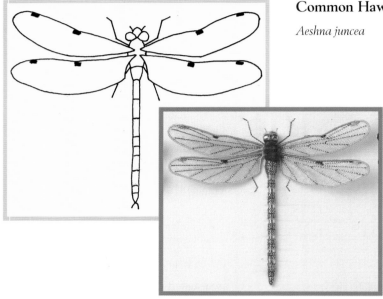

Order: Odonata

Suborder: Anisoptera

Family: Aeshnidae

These are the largest species in the order Odonata. Their characteristic hawk-like habit of constantly patrolling a territory gives hawker dragonflies their name.

The Hawker's territory is a stretch of river or lake, which the male defends against intruders. Male Hawkers are usually more brightly coloured than females. Wingspan $3\,^3/_4$" (95 mm); length 3" (76 mm).

Abdomen: Thread Wrapped Toothpick

                Gold metal plate

                Gold/black metallic thread

Wings: Four Detached   Gold metallic organza (upper layer)

                Gold mottled organza (lower layer)

                Fine gold silk thread (to overcast top edge)

                Light gold rayon machine thread

                Fine gold/black metallic thread (veins)

                Fine black metallic thread (pterostigma)

Thorax: Wrapped Chenille Thread

                Olive chenille thread

Head: Eyes, $^1/_8$" (3 mm) bronze/gold beads

                Mouthparts, gold silk thread

Legs/Antennae: Fine gold/black metallic thread

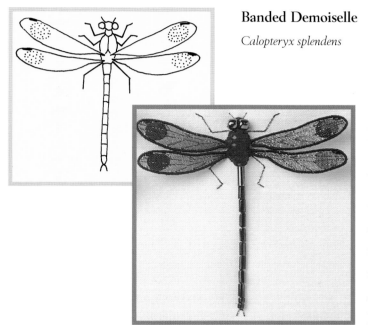

Banded Demoiselle

Calopteryx splendens

Order: Odonata

Suborder: Zygoptera

Family: Calopterygidae

With their delicate build, demoiselle damselflies flutter above the vegetation beside rivers and streams. When the insects are at rest, their wings are pressed together. The male has large blue patches on each of its four wings, and a polished-looking blue-brown body. Wingspan $2\,^5/_8''$ (65 mm); length $1\,^7/_8''$ (48 mm).

Abdomen: Beaded	Small blue/brown bugle beads and petite beads
	Fine green/charcoal metallic thread
Wings: Four Detached	Royal blue organza (upper layer)
	Pearl metal organdie (lower layer)
	Insert blue/black oval sequin shapes
	Royal blue rayon machine thread
	Fine gold/charcoal metallic thread (veins)
	Fine black metallic thread (pterostigma)
Thorax: Padded Leather	Black snake-skin (upside down for suede finish)
Head:	Eyes, $^1/_8''$ (3 mm) bronze/green beads
	Mouthparts, dark purple silk thread
Legs/Antennae:	Fine gold/charcoal metallic thread

Blue Damselfly

Diphlebia coerulescens

Order: Odonata
Suborder: Zygoptera
Family: Amphipterygidae

These large damselflies
like fast-flowing streams
and rivers, with an
abundance of vegetation.
They have dark-coloured
wings and a shiny
blue-brown abdomen.
Wingspan $2^3/4''$ (70 mm);
length 2″ (50 mm).

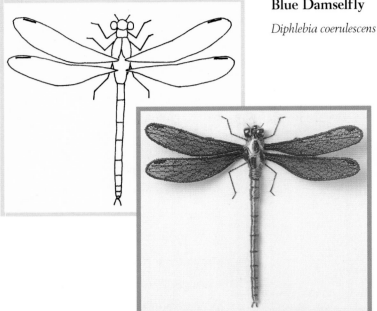

Abdomen: Thread Wrapped Pipe-cleaner

Variegated blue/brown rayon thread

Brown/black metallic thread

Wings: Four Detached Black voile coloured with gold oilstick (upper layer)

Fine black tulle (lower layer)

Black rayon machine thread

Fine brown/black metallic thread (veins)

Fine black metallic thread (pterostigma)

Thorax: Padded Leather Bronze snake-skin

Head: Eyes, $^1/_8''$ (3 mm) bronze beads

Mouthparts, petite bead

Legs/Antennae: Fine brown/black metallic thread

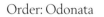

Red Skimmer Dragonfly

Libellula saturata

Order: Odonata

Suborder: Anisoptera

Family: Libellulidae

This dragonfly, which occurs on the west coast of the United States, has a flat, bright orange abdomen. The wings have copper-coloured wedges at the inner corners. They inhabit the banks of clean streams and rivers. Wingspan 3″ (76 mm); length 2″ (50 mm).

Abdomen: Padded Leather

Orange pig-skin padded with felt

Fine bronze/black metallic thread

Wings: Four Detached

Silver metallic organza (upper layer)

Pearl metal organdie (lower layer)

Insert circles of orange voile

Grey rayon machine thread

Fine bronze/black metallic thread (veins)

Fine black metallic thread (pterostigma)

Thorax: Wrapped Chenille Thread

Cinnamon chenille thread

Head:

Eyes, $^1/_8$″ (3 mm) bronze/wine beads

Mouthparts, dark purple silk thread

Legs/Antennae:

Fine bronze/black metallic thread

aue regina mater misericordie, vita dulcedo. Et spes nostra salue. Ad te clamamus
exules filij Eua. Ad te suspiramus gementes et flentes in hac lachrymarum valle. Eia ergo aduocata nostra illos tuos misericordes oculos ad nos conuerte. Et Jesum benedictum fruc-
tum ventris tui nobis post hoc exilium ostende. O clemens, o pia, o dulcis Virgo Maria. ora pro
nobis sancta dei genetrix. Vt digni efficiamur promissionibus Christi. Omnipotens sem-
piterne deus, qui gloriose virginis matris Maria corpus et animam, ut dignum filij tui ha-
baculum effici mereretur spiritu sancto cooperante praeparasti, da ut cuius commemo-
ratione laetamur eius pia intercessione, ab instantibus malis, et a morte perpetua libe-
remur. Amen:

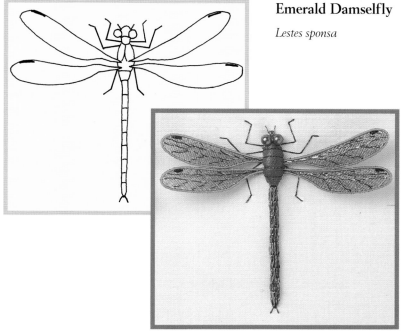

Emerald Damselfly

Lestes sponsa

Order: Odonata

Suborder: Zygoptera

Family: Lestidae

The slender body and transparent wings of these damselflies, makes them almost invisible when they settle – after a short flight – onto aquatic plants and shrubs. The Emerald Damselfly, with its slim, green abdomen, is the most common species. They frequent ponds, pools and stagnant water. Wingspan $1\,^3/_4''$ (45 mm); length $1^1/_2''$ (38 mm).

Abdomen: Raised Stem Stitch Band

    Green rayon and peacock-green blending filament worked together

Wings: Four Detached   Green organza (upper layer)

    Blue/bronze metallic organdie (lower layer)

    Green rayon machine thread

    Peacock-green blending filament (veins)

    Fine black metallic thread (pterostigma)

Thorax: Padded Leather   Olive leather couched with

    Fine brown/black metallic thread

Head: Eyes, $^1/_8''$ (3 mm) terracotta 'pearl' beads

    Mouthparts, petite bead

Legs/Antennae: Fine brown/black metallic thread

HOW TO EMBROIDER A STUMPWORK DRAGONFLY

he fun of embroidery lies in experimenting - experimenting with techniques, with patterns, with materials - saying "Let's have a go and try this", and if it does not suit, working out an alternative method, in a new colour scheme and on a slightly different scale.

(Beck 1997, p. 11)

This comment, made by Thomasina Beck, perfectly describes this chapter. There are so many ways that an embroidered dragonfly's wings, abdomen and thorax can be worked. It has been great fun experimenting and the results are set out here.

A dragonfly can be worked on almost any type of background fabric; silk, satin, linen, velvet, suede, even silk paper.

Preparation

1. Mount a 6" (15 cm) square of main fabric, with a square of quilter's muslin (or calico) as a backing, into a 4" embroidery hoop. The fabrics need to be kept very taut.

2. Trace a skeleton outline of the dragonfly onto tracing paper with an HB lead pencil. Flip the paper over and draw over the outline on the back.

3. Tape the tracing, right side up, to the fabric in the hoop. Place a small, circular board (or lid) inside the back of the hoop for support, then transfer the design using a stylus, empty ballpoint pen or a pencil.

Hints:

- I use GLAD Bake (baking parchment) for tracing paper.
- Only trace the abdomen and wing application points (a skeleton outline) onto the front of the fabric. If the wing positions (for appliquéd wings), or leg positions are required, trace them onto the muslin backing (the lines may show if they are traced onto the main fabric).
- If the fabric is dark, patterned or textured, transfer the design to the muslin backing and thread-trace (with a line of tacking stitches) through to the front.

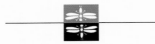

A dragonfly is usually embroidered in the following order; the abdomen, wings, thorax, head and finally the legs. There are several alternative methods provided for each of these. Select the one appropriate to the project you are working.

To work the abdomen

Use beads, thread or leather to work the abdomen – the variations are endless.

Method One

Beaded (e.g. *Banded Demoiselle*)

Stitch a beaded abdomen, curved or straight, with the beads of your choice.

You will need:

* The appropriate number of bugle beads and petite beads for the abdomen you are working

* Fine nylon, rayon or metallic thread in a size 12 Sharps or Beading needle

1. Secure the thread to the backing fabric and bring the needle up at A. Thread on the bugle beads, then the petite beads and insert the needle at B (make sure that the length of the stitch is longer than the combined length of the beads so that the beads will sit smoothly). Bring the needle up at C, then couch over the thread between each bead back to B (over the traced line). Take the needle back through all the beads to A and secure.

2. With the desired thread in the needle, work a fly stitch for the cerci (tail), then bring the 'tie-down' thread back through all the beads to A and secure.

Method Two

Raised Stem Stitch Band (e.g. *Ruddy Darter*)

Work raised stem stitch with a variegated thread for an interesting effect, or combine a plain thread with a blending filament. For a stripy body, work rows of alternate colours. The body can be curved or straight.

You will need:

· Stranded cotton, silk or rayon – one strand in a size 10 Crewel needle

· Soft cotton thread (e.g. DMC Tapestry Cotton) in a matching colour – one strand in a size 18 Chenille needle

· A size 26 Tapestry needle

1. Pad the abdomen with two strands of soft cotton thread. Bring the needle up at A and down at B, temporarily securing the tails of thread on the back with masking tape (keep clear of the abdomen).

2. Using the stranded thread, couch the padding in place over the traced line, with the appropriate number of stitches, then secure. To obtain a slender, rounded abdomen, it is important that each couching stitch comes up and returns at the same point.

3. With the stranded thread in the Tapestry needle, come up at A and work raised stem stitch over the couching stitches, going down at B. Work as many rows as required to cover the padding. Trim the tails of the padding thread at the back.

2. Cross-section of couching stitch

4. Optional: couch again, firmly, over the stitched abdomen, placing the couching stitches between the previous ones to form segments. This looks effective in metallic thread.

5. Embroider the tail with small back stitches, chain stitches or a fly stitch.

Method Three Leather

There are two ways that fine kid leather, suede or snakeskin can be used to form a dragonfly's abdomen.

(a) Leather padded with felt (e.g. *Broad-bodied Chaser*)

 You will need:

· Fine kid leather, suede or snakeskin

· Felt and Vliesofix (paper-backed fusible web) for padding

· One strand of matching thread in a size 10 Crewel needle

· Fine metallic thread in a size 9 Straw/milliners needle

1. Draw the abdomen shape onto Vliesofix, fuse to the felt then cut out the shape.

2. Fuse the felt shape to the back of the leather, then cut out a leather shape $^1/_8''$ (3 mm) larger all round than the felt.

3. Fold in the $^1/_8''$ (3 mm) turning and catch together at the back with the stranded thread. Squeeze the lower point with tweezers.

4. Apply the padded leather shape to the fabric with ten couching stitches using metallic thread, then ease the needle under the couching stitches to form a long stitch from the thorax to the tail.

5. Work the cerci (tail) with a fly stitch.

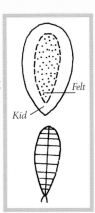

(b) Leather wrapped around a toothpick (e.g. *Club-tailed Dragonfly*)

You will need:

· A toothpick and stranded cotton

· Fine snakeskin

· Fabric glue

· Fine metallic thread in a size 9 Straw/milliners needle

50

1. Wrap the toothpick with one strand of cotton to form a club shape near the pointed end. Cut the toothpick to the required length.

2. Attach the toothpick to the back of the snakeskin with a tiny amount of glue. Cut out the snakeskin leaving enough turning on each side to wrap and meet at the back of the toothpick. Secure with glue. Squeeze the lower point with tweezers.

3. Apply the wrapped shape to the fabric with ten couching stitches using metallic thread. It is not possible to stitch the cerci as the tail is above the fabric.

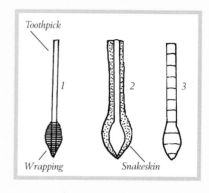

Method Four Wrapping

Wood, fine cord or wire can be wrapped with a variety of threads to produce an interesting abdomen.

(a) Wrapped toothpick (e.g. *Common Hawker*)

You will need:

· A toothpick and double-sided adhesive tape

· Metal plate, flat metallic thread or gold paint

· Contrasting metallic thread an appropriate Straw/milliners needle

· Fine metallic thread in a size 9 Straw/milliners needle

1. Cut the toothpick to the required length and cover with a narrow strip of tape.

2. Wrap the toothpick with metal plate or flat metallic thread, leaving the tail

uncovered. Alternatively, the toothpick may be painted with gold paint.

3. Wrap bands of contrasting metallic thread along the abdomen, securing each band with a buttonhole stitch before proceeding to the next band. Commence wrapping at the tail, enclosing the end of the thread.

4. Apply the wrapped toothpick to the fabric with couching stitches worked at each band, using fine metallic thread. It is not possible to stitch the cerci as the tail sits above the fabric.

(b) Wrapped pipe-cleaner (e.g. *Blue Damselfly*)

You will need:

· A pipe-cleaner

· Stranded cotton or rayon thread for wrapping – variegated thread is lovely

· Fine metallic thread in a size 9 Straw/milliners needle

1. Cut the pipe-cleaner slightly longer than required. Remove some of the tufts from each end before wrapping.

2. Using one strand of thread, wrap the pipe-cleaner until it is the required thickness. Do not wrap the ends.

3. Apply the wrapped pipe-cleaner to the fabric with ten couching stitches using metallic thread. Before couching, use a large yarn darner to insert the wire ends through to the back. Secure.

4. Work the cerci (tail) with a fly stitch.

To work the wings

Gauzy, wired, detached wings are a delightful characteristic of stumpwork dragonflies. The wings can also be worked on the surface of the fabric.

Almost any sheer, organza-like fabric or ribbon (plain, 'shot', variegated, metallic or pearlised) can be used for the upper layer of the wings. Use similar fabrics for the lower layer, or a more opaque pearl, gold or copper metal organdie, which provides a lovely sheen under the sheer organzas.

Method One Four Detached Wings (e.g. *Dragonfly and Viburnum*)

You will need:

· 4″ embroidery hoop

· 6″ (15 cm) square of organza for the upper layer

· 6″ (15 cm) square of organza or organdie for the lower layer

· 6″ (15 cm) square of Vliesofix (paper-backed fusible web)

· GLAD Bake (baking parchment)

- 28 gauge uncovered cake decorator's wire (cut into 4 $^3/_4$" or 12 cm lengths)
- Fine tweezers (try surgical tweezers)
- Madeira Rayon No. 40 machine embroidery thread in a size 12 Sharps needle (or a size 10 Crewel needle)
- Fine metallic thread or blending filament in a size 9 Straw/milliners needle
- A size 14 Yarn Darner needle to apply the wings

1. A wing 'sandwich' is made by fusing the upper and lower layers of fabric together with Vliesofix. If using ribbon as the upper layer, remove the selvedges, and cut the Vliesofix to the same width. Place one layer of fabric on the bias/cross-grain for a pretty effect. Protect the ironing board and iron with sheets of GLAD Bake.

(a) Fuse the Vliesofix to the upper fabric, then remove the backing paper.

(b) Place the lower fabric (over GLAD Bake) on the ironing board.

(c) Place the upper fabric, on the bias, glue-side down, over the lower layer.

(d) Cover the 'sandwich' with GLAD Bake and press firmly with an iron (on about Nylon setting). The temperature needs to be hot enough to fuse the fabrics but not so hot as to cause bubbling.

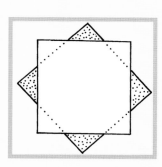

   Mount the wing 'sandwich' into a 4" embroidery hoop. The fabric needs to be kept very taut.

2. Bend the wires into the two wing shapes, using the diagrams provided as a guide. To do this, lay the wire over the diagram and temporarily secure one end to the paper at *, with a small piece of masking tape. Use the tweezers to bend the wire into

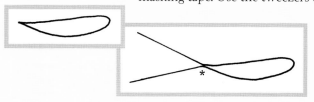

shape, using your fingers to keep it in place as you bend it. Work back to *. Leave two tails of wire for each wing and do not cross the wires at *.

3. Using one strand of rayon thread, stitch the wire to the wing 'sandwich' in the hoop, with small and close overcasting stitches, starting and ending at * with a few stitches over both wires. It is helpful to hold the wire temporarily in place on the hoop with a small piece of masking tape. Work two front wings and two back wings, making sure that you have a right and a left wing for each.

Stitch
Wire
Fabric

Cross-section
of overcasting stitch

Hints:

* When overcasting, it is important to make your stitches close to the wire with an up and down stabbing motion, to avoid 'wayward' stitches. Pull each stitch quite firmly.

* If you need to renew a thread while overcasting the wing, do not use a knot. Instead, hold the tail of the old thread and the tail of the new thread under the length of wire about to be stitched. Catch both tails of thread in with the new overcasting stitches.

4. Work the veins in each wing in feather stitch or single feather stitch with metallic thread or blending filament, using the diagram as a guide. It is safer to keep the tails of thread at the front of the wing until it has been cut out, then stitch the threads through to the back of the wing. The tails of thread are secured after the wing has been applied to the main fabric.

5. To embroider the pterostigma (opaque wing markings) in the top corner of each wing, work three satin stitches on top of each other in metallic thread, knotting the tails of thread together at the back. This step is optional.

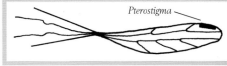

Pterostigma

6. With sharp scissors, carefully cut out the wings, avoiding the tails of thread. If you happen to snip a stitch (it happens), repair by applying a minute amount of PVA glue with the point of a pin.

7. Before applying a pair of wings, hold both wings together and bend the wire tails at right angles to ensure that they are the same length.

8. The wings are applied to the main fabric by inserting the wire tails through a 'tunnel' formed by the eye of a large Yarn Darner needle.

(a) Pierce the main fabric, at the point marked at the top of the abdomen, with the large Yarn Darner, and push it through until the eye is halfway through the fabric.

(b) Insert the wire and thread tails of the back wings through the 'tunnel' formed by the eye of the needle, to the back of the work.

(c) Gently pull the needle all the way through, leaving the wire and threads in the hole (the wires and thread tails can be inserted in two movements if desired).

(d) Bend the wire and thread tails under the abdomen and hold in place temporarily with masking tape. Repeat the process to apply the front wings.

(e) Secure the wires to the muslin backing behind the abdomen with small stitches, using a single strand of thread. Trim the wires to different lengths to reduce the bulk (use wire cutters or old scissors). Do not let any wire protrude past the cerci.

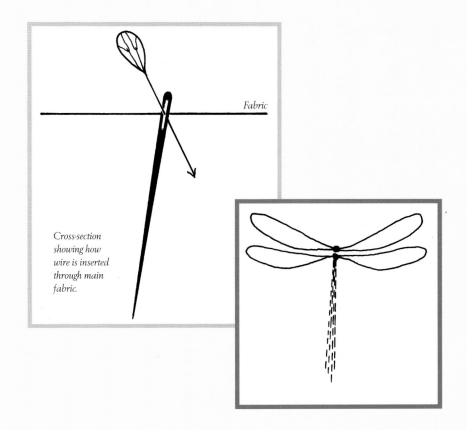

Fabric

Cross-section showing how wire is inserted through main fabric.

Extra Embellishment for Detached Wings

Layering fabrics without the use of Vliesofix can make a more delicate wing 'sandwich'. Use this method if you wish to insert an embellishment between the wing layers, or if you are using tulle as the lower layer.

(a) To insert shapes of contrasting fabric:

Dragonflies, such as the *Red Skimmer Dragonfly*, have wedges of contrasting colour at the inner corners of their wings, which can be achieved by inserting circles of

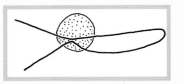

contrasting fabric between the upper and lower layers of the wing 'sandwich'. Fuse a small piece of Vliesofix to the contrasting fabric. Cut out the desired circles or shapes and fuse to the lower layer of wing fabric. Cover the lower layer, and the shapes, with the upper layer of wing fabric and mount into the hoop. Place wires so that a segment of contrasting colour appears in the corner of the wings. Proceed as before with stitching and cutting.

(b) To insert sequin shapes:

Some dragonflies, e.g. *Banded Demoiselle*, have patches of shimmering colour near the tips of their wings. To achieve this, insert ovals of sequin between the upper and lower layers of the wing 'sandwich'. Carefully cut out appropriately sized ovals from large, flat sequins, insert loosely between the layers of the wing 'sandwich', and mount into the hoop. Stitch one side of the wing wire to the fabric, then ease the sequin into place by tapping the hoop or nudging with a needle from the back. Continue stitching around the wire, enclosing the sequin.

(c) Tulle as the lower layer:

Use fine tulle or lace as the lower layer of the wing, e.g. *Blue Damselfly*. If the lace is not wide enough to fit in the hoop, stitch a strip of scrap fabric to each side. To obtain an interesting result, it is important that the mesh of the tulle or lace is tiny.

Method Two Four Appliquéd Wings

This method of working dragonfly's wings is useful if you are embroidering an object that needs to be more robust, e.g. a book cover or a handbag mirror. When working a dragonfly with this method, apply the wings before working the abdomen.

You will need:

· Organza for the upper layer

· Organdie for the lower layer (optional)

· Vliesofix (paper-backed fusible web)

· Rayon machine thread in a size 12 Sharps needle (for some projects)

· Fine metallic thread or blending filament in a size 9 Straw/milliners needle

· Nylon thread in a size 12 Sharps needle

1. Prepare the wing sandwich as for detached wings, or use a single layer of fabric.

2. Trace four wing outlines onto the paper-side of Vliesofix. Make sure that you have a right and left front wing, and a right and left back wing.

3. Fuse the traced Vliesofix to the back of the wing 'sandwich'. Use GLAD Bake to protect the iron and ironing board.

4. Carefully cut out the wing shapes, remove the paper backing, then fuse the wings into position on the main fabric. Use fine needles, inserted along the traced lines from the back, to indicate the wing positions – remove before you iron. Use a small round board or lid under the hoop to support the fabric, and GLAD Bake to protect the fabric and the iron.

5. Stitch an outline around the wing.

(a) Work a row of split back stitch at the edge of the wing with rayon thread, or

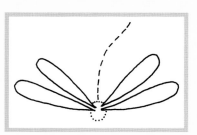

(b) Couch metallic thread around the outside edge of each wing, using nylon thread for the couching stitches. Work these stitches from the edge towards the wing to prevent the wing edge from lifting.

6. Work the veins and the pterostigma as for the detached wings.

Method Three Two Detached and Two Appliquéd Wings

Use this method if you are working a damselfly, viewed from the side, with two detached wings shadowing the two appliquéd wings, e.g. *Field Flowers and Damselfly*. Use the techniques as described previously, for both types of wings, and work in the following order:

(a) work appliquéd wings

(b) apply detached wings

(c) then work the abdomen

To work the thorax

Worked with chenille thread, padded leather, padded satin stitch or a large bead, the thorax covers the wing insertion points and connects to the top of the abdomen.

Method One Chenille Thread

Choose either the very fluffy silk chenille thread, available in plain colours, or the finer rayon chenille, with its extensive variegated colour options.

You will need:

· Chenille thread in a size 14 Yarn Darner needle

· One strand of cotton in a size 10 Crewel needle

There are two ways to embroider the thorax with chenille thread:

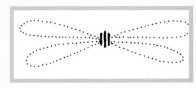

(a) e.g. *Dragonfly Handbag Mirror*. With one strand of chenille thread, work three straight stitches over the wing insertion points and connecting the abdomen. Take care not to twist the thread. The stitches need to be fairly loose and almost on top of each other. Secure the tails of chenille thread at the back with a few stitches in stranded thread.

(b) e.g. *Broad-bodied Chaser*. With one strand of chenille thread, work two straight stitches, as padding stitches, over the wing insertion points and connecting the abdomen. Cover these padding stitches with four or five wraps of chenille thread to represent segments. Take care not to twist the thread or to pull the wraps too tight. Secure the tails of chenille thread at the back with a few stitches in stranded thread.

Method Two Padded Leather e.g. *Variable Damselfly*

Use fine kid leather or snakeskin to work this very realistic thorax.

You will need:

· A small piece of snakeskin or kid leather
· Soft cotton thread or felt for padding
· Nylon thread in a size 12 Sharps needle
· Tweezers

1. Cut a small piece of snakeskin in the approximate shape of the thorax. It needs to be wide enough to cover the wires at the wing insertion points, and the top of the abdomen. You may need to experiment with the shape, trimming as you stitch.

2. Cut a small piece of felt, or work a few stitches in soft cotton thread to pad the centre of the thorax and prevent the snakeskin from collapsing.

3. Apply the snakeskin with a few (5-6) small stab stitches in nylon thread. Work the

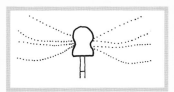

stitches from the main fabric into the edge of the snakeskin. The cut edges of the snakeskin are flush with the main fabric (in cross section

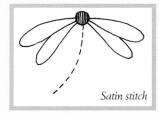

the snakeskin looks like ∩). Tweezers are helpful to shape the snakeskin around the wings and abdomen.

Other Thorax Methods

The thorax can also be

Satin stitch

worked in padded satin stitch (the stitches going over the wings), or with a large bead.

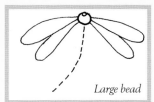

Large bead

To work the head

Huge eyes make up a large proportion of a dragonfly's head. Work these in beads, then add the antennae with fine metallic thread.

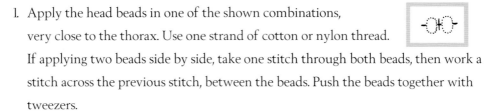

You will need:

· Beads in your choice of colour and size; petite beads, seed beads, $^1/_8$" (3 mm) and $^3/_{16}$" (4 mm) beads.
· Stranded cotton or nylon thread in a size 12 Sharps needle.
· Fine metallic thread in a size 9 Straw/milliners needle

1. Apply the head beads in one of the shown combinations, very close to the thorax. Use one strand of cotton or nylon thread. If applying two beads side by side, take one stitch through both beads, then work a stitch across the previous stitch, between the beads. Push the beads together with tweezers.
2. Work the antennae with straight stitches or a fly stitch, with a single strand of metallic thread.

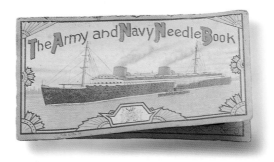

To work the legs

You will need fine metallic thread in a size 9 Straw/milliners needle.

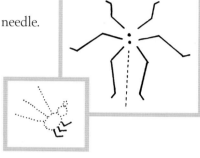

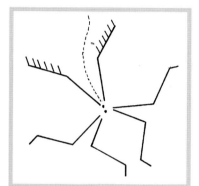

1. With a double strand of metallic thread, work three long back stitches for each leg, using the diagram, or the traced outline on the muslin backing, as a guide.

2. With one strand of metallic thread, work straight stitches for the 'spines' on the back legs, if desired.

3. If you wish to make the legs very long, as seen in some seventeenth century embroidered dragonflies, secure these long stitches with couching stitches in metallic thread.

PROJECTS

When embroidering dragonflies, the choices are numerous. In each of the following projects, the dragonfly is worked in a different way. Experiment, and feel free to change any aspect of the design, including the size.

Please note:

The diagrams at the beginning of each project are accurate in size. The explanatory drawings accompanying the instructions may not be true to scale.

Detailed instructions are provided for each project except for the working of the dragonfly, which can be found in the chapter, 'How to Work a Stumpwork Dragonfly'.

Equipment

The stumpwork embroiderer's workbox should contain the following equipment:

- Good quality embroidery hoops – 4″, 6″ and 9″
- Needles: Crewel/Embroidery sizes 3 – 10   Straw/Milliners sizes 1 – 10

   Sharps sizes 10 – 12   Tapestry sizes 24 – 28

   Chenille sizes 18 – 24   Yarn Darner size 14
- Scissors - small, with sharp points
- Thimble
- Pins - fine glass-headed pins
- Small wire cutters or old scissors
- Fine tweezers (from surgical suppliers)
- Eyebrow comb (for Turkey knots)
- Screwdriver (for tightening the embroidery hoop)
- Tracing paper (I use GLAD Bake/baking parchment)
- Fine ($^{1}/_{32}$″ or 0.5 mm) HB lead pencil (mechanical)
- Stylus or empty ballpoint pen (for tracing)
- Masking tape
- 'Ideas' notebook

Dragonfly and Viburnum

Requirements

- 5" or 6" embroidery hoop
- 4" embroidery hoop
- Tracing paper (GLAD Bake) − 6" (15 cm) square
- Ivory satin − 8" (20 cm) square
- Quilters' muslin/calico − 8" (20 cm) square
- Green mottled organza − 6" (15 cm) square
- Pearl organdie − 6" (15 cm) square
- Vliesofix (paper-backed fusible web) − 6" (15 cm) square
- Uncovered cake decorators' wire − 28 gauge (cut in 4 $^3/_4$" or 12 cm lengths)

- Needles: - Crewel/Embroidery sizes 9 and 10
  - Straw/Milliners sizes 1 and 9
  - Sharps size 12 or Beading size 12
  - Yarn Darner size 14

- Beads: - Mill Hill Small Bugle Beads 70374 (Dark Teal colour)
  - Mill Hill Petite Beads 40374 (Dark Teal colour)
  - Mill Hill Seed Beads 374 (Dark Teal colour)
  - $^3/_{16}$" (4 mm) glass bead (Hot Spotz SBX6-449)
  - Mill Hill Glass Seed Beads 145, 2005 (light and medium pink)

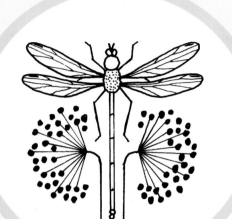

- Threads:

  Viburnum

  - Pink stranded (DMC 818, 776, 3326, 899, 335)
  - Green stranded (DMC 3363)

  Dragonfly

  – Green rayon machine embroidery (Madeira Rayon No.40 colour 1047)
    – Nylon clear thread
      – Peacock-green blending filament (Kreinik Blending Filament 085)
        – Black blending filament (Madeira Metallic No.40 colour 70)
        – Gold/black metallic (Kreinik Cord 205c)
        – Dark green chenille thread (Hunter-olive variegated chenille)
      – Dark navy stranded (DMC 939)

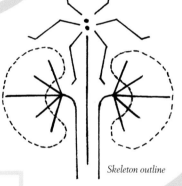

Skeleton outline

Front wing shape

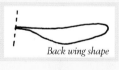

Back wing shape

Abdomen and wing placement points

This project can be framed, or mounted into the lid of a small (3″) Framecraft gilt pincushion, or inserted into a large (3$^1/_2$″) Framecraft paperweight with a recessed wooden base.

Order of work

1. Preparation

Mount the satin and muslin backing into a 5" or 6" embroidery hoop, stretching both fabrics tight. Trace the skeleton outline onto tracing paper with an HB lead pencil. Flip the paper over, centre the design over the muslin backing (lead pencil side down), and secure the edges with a little masking tape to prevent slipping. Draw over the lines with an empty ballpoint pen or a pencil, to transfer the design onto the muslin.

2. Viburnum Stems and Branches

Following the traced outline, tack the stems with one strand of green thread (3363). Embroider the stems in whipped chain stitch with two strands of thread. Work the row of chain stitch from the base of the stem, removing the tacking stitches as you go, then whip. The branches are straight stitches worked with one strand of thread. Work five straight stitches as marked on the tracing, then add eight more stitches of varying lengths (thirteen altogether on each side).

3. Viburnum Flower

Fill each flower shape with beads and French knots, working some at the end of the branches and scattering some within the traced outline. Work the French knots with six strands of thread and one wrap, using the size 1 Straw needle. Work five knots in each pink (818, 776, 3326, 899, 335), then apply the beads, about seven of each colour, using one strand of thread and two small stitches for each bead. Work about another five knots in each colour.

4. Dragonfly Abdomen

Following the instructions for Abdomen, Method One (page 48), use one strand of nylon thread in the size 12 Sharps needle, to work the abdomen with five bugle beads (70374) and two petite beads (40374). Use a double strand of peacock blending filament in the size 12 Sharps needle to work the fly stitch and 'tie-down'.

5. Detached Dragonfly Wings

Work and apply four detached wings following the instructions for Wing, Method One (page 52). Fuse the green mottled organza to the pearl organdie backing, one layer on the bias/cross grain. Mount the wing 'sandwich', green side up, into the 4" embroidery hoop.

Bend the wires into the two wing shapes, using the diagrams provided as a guide. Using one strand of green rayon thread (1047) in the size 12 Sharps (or size 10 Crewel) needle, stitch the wire to the fabric. Work two front and two back wings, making sure that you have a right and a left side wing for each.

Work the veins in each wing in single feather stitch, using one strand of peacock blending filament in the size 9 Straw needle. Embroider the pterostigma, using one strand of black blending filament in the size 9 Straw needle.

Carefully cut out the wings, then stitch the thread tails through to the back. Bend the wire tails of the wings at right angles before inserting both the back wings at D and both the front wings at E.

6. The Thorax

The thorax is worked with one strand of chenille thread in the Yarn Darner needle. Work two padding stitches over the wing insertion points, then cover the padding stitches with four or five wraps (see (b) page 58).

7. The Head

Using one strand of dark navy thread, apply one $^3/_{16}$" (4 mm) bead for the head, stitching with the hole towards the thorax. To work the eyes, apply two seed beads (347) together (from side to side), with two straight stitches, close to the head. Finish with one straight stitch between the beads towards the head to make the beads sit evenly.

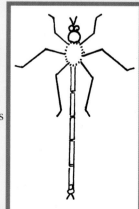

8. The Legs

Using two strands of gold/black metallic cord in the size 9 Straw needle, work three back stitches for each leg using the tracing on the back as a guide. Work a fly stitch for the antennae with a single strand of thread.

Dragonfly Handbag Mirror

Requirements

- 4″ embroidery hoop
- Tracing paper (GLAD Bake) – 6″ (15 cm) square
- Ivory silk – 6″ (15 cm) square
- Quilters' muslin/calico – 6″ (15 cm) square
- Olive green organza ribbon – 6″ (15 cm)
- Pearl organdie – 6″ (15 cm) square
- Vliesofix (paper-backed fusible web) – 6″ (15 cm) square

- Needles: - Crewel/Embroidery size 10
  - Tapestry size 26
  - Straw/Milliners size 9
  - Chenille size 20
  - Yarn Darner size 14

- Beads: - Mill Hill Seed Beads 374 (Dark Teal colour)
  - $3/16$″ (4 mm) glass bead (Hot Spotz SBX6-449)

- Threads: - Peacock-green blending filament (Kreinik Blending Filament 085)
  - Nylon clear thread
  - Brown soft cotton (DMC Tapestry Cotton 2730)
  - Variegated brown/green stranded (Needle Necessities Overdyed 130)
  - Dark green chenille thread (Au Ver à Soie Chenille à Broder 2126)
  - Bronze/black metallic (Kreinik Cord 215c)

This project can be mounted into the back of a Framecraft Handbag Mirror.

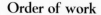

Order of work

1. Preparation

Mount the silk and muslin backing into a 4″ embroidery hoop, stretching both fabrics tight. Trace the skeleton outline onto tracing paper with an HB lead pencil. Flip the paper over, centre the design over the calico backing (lead pencil side down), and secure the edges with a little masking tape to prevent slipping. Draw over the lines with an empty ballpoint pen or a pencil, to transfer the design onto the muslin.

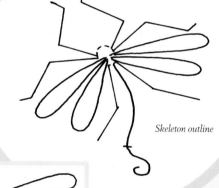

Skeleton outline

2. Appliquéd Dragonfly Wings

Apply four wings to the silk following the instructions for Appliquéd Wings (page 57).

Fuse the green organza ribbon to the pearl organdie backing, one layer on the bias/cross grain.

Cut out four wing shapes and

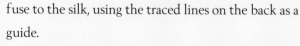

Veins

fuse to the silk, using the traced lines on the back as a guide.

Couch a line of peacock-green blending filament around the outside edge of each wing, using nylon thread, in a size 12 Sharps needle, to work the couching stitches.

Work the veins in each wing in feather stitch, using one strand of peacock blending filament in a size 9 Straw needle.

3. Dragonfly Abdomen

Following the instructions for Abdomen, Method Two (page 49), work the abdomen in raised stem stitch band.

Pad the abdomen with two strands of soft cotton thread (2730) using the size 20 chenille needle. Following the traced line on the back, couch the padding in place with eight stitches, using one strand of variegated thread in a size 10 Crewel needle. Using the same variegated thread in a size 26 Tapestry needle, work raised stem stitch over the couching stitches to cover the padding.

Couch again, firmly, over the stitched abdomen, placing the couching stitches between the previous ones, to form segments.

Embroider the tail with small chain stitches.

4. The Thorax

With one strand of chenille thread, work three straight stitches over the wing insertion points, at the top of the abdomen. (see (a) page 58).

5. The Head

Apply a $^3/_{16}$" (4 mm) bead for the head, stitching with the hole towards the thorax (in the sample, I have used a mis-shapen $^3/_{16}$" or 4 mm bead). To work the eyes, apply two seed beads (347), one on either side of the head.

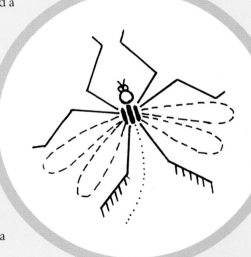

6. The Legs

Using two strands of bronze/black metallic thread in a size 9 Straw needle, work three back stitches for each leg, using the tracing on the back as a guide. With one strand of metallic thread, work straight stitches for spines on the back legs, and a fly stitch for the antennae.

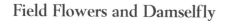

Field Flowers and Damselfly

Requirements

- 4″ embroidery hoops
- 5″ or 6″ embroidery hoop
- Tracing paper (GLAD Bake) – 6″ (15 cm) square
- Ivory satin – 8″ (20 cm) square
- Quilter's muslin/calico - three 8″ (20 cm) squares
- Bronze organza – 6″ (15 cm) square
- Paper-backed fusible web (Vliesofix) – 6″ (15 cm) square
- Grey felt – two pieces (3″ x 2″)
- Paper-backed fusible web – three pieces (3″ x 2″)
- Bronze kid or snakeskin – small piece
- Wire: - 28 gauge uncovered wire (cut in 4 3/4″ or 12 cm lengths)
  - 30 gauge green covered wire (7 ″ or 18 cm length)
  - fine flower wire (cut in 4 3/4″ or 12 cm lengths)
- Red marking pen to colour the flower wire (optional)
- Needles: - Crewel/Embroidery sizes 5–10
  - Straw/Milliners sizes 3–9
  - Sharps size 12 or Beading size 12
  - Tapestry size 26
  - Yarn Darner size 14
- Beads: - Mill Hill Small Bugle Beads 72053 (nutmeg)
  - Mill Hill Petite Beads 42024 (nutmeg)
  - Mill Hill Petite Beads 40374 (Dark Teal colour)
  - 1/8″ (3 mm) glass bead (Hot Spotz SBXL-449 Dark Teal colour)

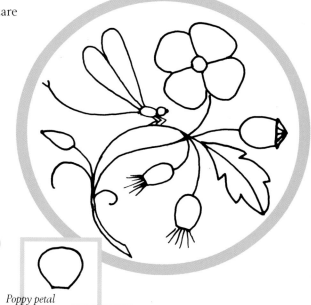

Poppy petal

Damselfly wings

71

- Threads:

    Oriental Poppy

        - Red stranded (Madeira Silk 210 or DMC 666)

        - Dark purple or black stranded (Soie d'Alger 3326 or DMC 310)

        - Dark plum stranded (Soie d'Alger 4636 or DMC 3802)

        - Green Pearl (8) thread (DMC 3348)

        - Dark, medium and light green stranded (DMC 3345, 3346, 3347)

        - Very pale green (DMC 472)

    Centaurea (perennial cornflower)

        - Blue/purple stranded (DMC 791, 792 and/or Madeira Silk 903)

        - Green stranded (DMC 3362)

    Damselfly

        - Bronze rayon machine embroidery (Madeira Rayon No.40 colour 1057)

        - Peacock-green metallic filament (Kreinik Blending Filament colour 085)

        - Bronze/black metallic (Kreinik Cord 215c)

        - Nylon clear thread

Skeleton outline

Order of work

1. Preparation

Mount the satin and muslin backing into a 5" or 6" embroidery hoop, stretching both fabrics tight. Trace the skeleton outline onto tracing paper with an HB lead pencil, flip the paper over and draw over the outline on the back. Centre the tracing, right side up, over the satin in the hoop, and secure the edges with a little masking tape to prevent slipping. Place a small, circular board or lid inside the back of the hoop for support, then draw over the lines with an empty ballpoint pen or a pencil to transfer the design.

2. Poppy Stems and Leaves

The poppy stems are worked in stem stitch using two strands of dark green thread (3345). Starting at the base, work two rows of stem stitch side by side (only one line is drawn on the skeleton outline), then continue one row to the flower and one row to the seed pod. The lower curved tendril is worked in stem stitch with one strand of mid-green thread (3346).

Embroider the leaf on the main fabric with one strand of thread as follows:

- central vein in chain stitch (3347)
- leaf surface in long and short stitch (3346)
- side veins with straight stitches (3347)

Work the detached leaf, on muslin/calico mounted in a 4" hoop, as follows:

- couch then overcast green covered wire down central vein (3347)
- bend, couch then buttonhole the wire around the outside edge (3346)
- embroider the leaf surface in long and short stitch (3346)
- work the veins with straight stitches (3347)

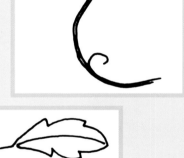

3. Poppy Seed Pod

Using paper-backed fusible web (Vliesofix), cut three pieces of grey felt to pad the seed pod, one the actual shape of the pod and two successively smaller. With one strand of green thread (3347), stab stitch the smaller shapes in place, then apply and outline the larger shape with buttonhole stitch. Using the same thread, cover the pod with satin stitch, working the stitches closer together at the base to give a realistic shape.

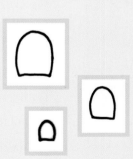

The top of the pod is worked in whipped spider web stitch. Work three stitches with the pearl thread (3348) to form the five foundation spokes $^1/_{32}$" (1 mm) into the satin stitched base as shown, holding the pearl thread at point ∗ until the whipping is complete. With one strand of pale green stranded thread (472) in a crewel needle, work the pod in whipped spider web stitch, starting at ∗ and inserting the needle through the fabric at the beginning and end of each row (use the eye of the needle when whipping). When filled, take the pearl thread to the back of the work at point ∗ and secure. Work a French knot over point ∗ with pale green thread if desired.

To form a ridge at the base of the pod, work a bullion knot with one strand of green (3347) thread in a Straw needle.

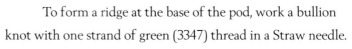

Bullion knot

4. Cornflower Stems and Cornflowers

The cornflower stems are embroidered in chain stitch with two strands of green thread (3362). Work the lower curved stem first, then the main stem, changing to one strand of thread when it branches into three and crosses the poppy stems. Work the cornflower bud stem with one strand of thread.

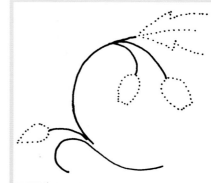

Cornflowers: Using paper-backed fusible web, cut two layers of grey felt to pad each cornflower base – one the actual size and one slightly smaller. With one strand of green thread (3362), stab stitch the smaller layer of felt in place, then apply and outline the larger shape with buttonhole stitch.

Starting at the top of the base (straight edge), cover the felt (and outline) in corded detached buttonhole stitch, using one strand of green thread in a crewel needle. The laid threads (cord) are worked from left to right (using the point of the needle), and the detached buttonhole stitches are worked from left to right (using the eye of the needle), as shown in the diagram. Increase or decrease stitches at the beginning and end of rows as required.

1. straight stitch (cord) •——————→ •

2. detached buttonhole •eeeeeeeee→•

3. straight stitch (cord) •——————→ •

4. detached buttonhole over cord and into loops of row above •eeeeeeee→ •

5. straight stitch (cord) •——————→ •

– and so on

Work the cornflower petals in Turkey knots (about six to eight rows), using two strands of thread, mixing the colours randomly. Cut and comb the pile to achieve the desired effect.

Cornflower Bud: Using paper-backed fusible web, cut one layer of grey felt to pad the cornflower bud. With one strand of green thread, apply and outline the shape with buttonhole stitch. Cover the felt (and outline) in corded detached buttonhole stitch as for the cornflowers, working the first laid thread (cord) a little way down from the tip of the bud. Embroider the tip of the bud with straight stitches in green or purple thread, or work a few Turkey knots.

5. Poppy Flower

With one strand of red thread, embroider the outside edge of the poppy petals on the main fabric in long and short buttonhole stitch (work the stitches close together, keeping the stitch direction towards the centre of the poppy). Embroider the petals in red with long and short stitches, leaving a space for the 'blotch' at the base. Work the 'blotch' in dark purple or black. Leave a small gap ($1/32$" or 1 mm) between the embroidery and the centre outline, in which to insert the detached petals.

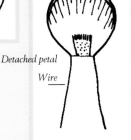

Detached petal

Wire

To work the detached poppy petals, mount muslin/calico into a hoop and trace four petal outlines (see page 71).

Colour the flower wire with red marking pen, if desired. With one strand of red thread, couch then buttonhole the flower wire around the outside edge of the petal, leaving two tails of wire. Work a row of long and short buttonhole stitch inside the petal, close to the wire (work stitches close together, keeping the stitch direction towards the centre of the poppy). Embroider each petal and the 'blotches' as for the petals on the main fabric.

Carefully cut out the detached petals and apply them to the main fabric, inserting the wires from each petal through two holes, using the chenille needle. As poppy petals occur in 'pairs', apply the petals, two at a time, opposite each other around the centre outline. Bend the wire underneath each petal at the back of the work and secure with tiny stitches. Trim the wire.

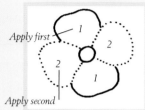

The centre of the poppy is worked in whipped spider web stitch. Using the pearl thread (3348), work four long stitches, crossing each other in the centre and extending into the petals, to form a foundation (spokes) for the whipping. Hold these threads together in the centre with a spare piece of thread. Work a whipped spider web over

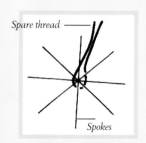

these foundation stitches with one strand of dark plum thread in the tapestry needle, pulling gently on the spare thread as you whip, causing the web to be slightly raised. When whipping is complete, remove the spare thread revealing the small green centre point. With two strands of dark purple or black thread (or one of each), work sixteen Turkey knots around the

whipped centre for stamen (one knot at the end of each spoke and one in between), then cut to the desired length. Shape the petals with tweezers.

6. Damselfly Wings

Fuse the bronze organza to the pearl organdie backing, one layer on the bias/cross grain. Use the edge of this wing 'sandwich' for the applied wings.

Apply two wings to the satin following the instructions for Appliquéd Wings (page 58), using the two wing outlines on page 71.

Cut out an upper and lower wing, using the diagram as a guide, and fuse to the main fabric at A. To outline the edge of the fused wings, work a row of split back stitch using one strand of bronze rayon thread (1057) in a size 12 Sharps needle. Work the veins in each wing in feather stitch, using one strand of peacock blending filament in a size 9 Straw needle.

Work and apply two detached wings following the instructions for Wing Method One (page 52). Mount the remainder of the wing 'sandwich', bronze side up, into a 4" embroidery hoop.

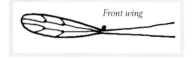

Front wing

Bend the wires into the two wing shapes, using the diagrams provided as a guide. Using one strand of bronze rayon thread in the size 12 Sharps (or size 10 Crewel) needle, stitch the wire to the fabric. Work one front and one back wing. Work the veins in each wing in single feather stitch, using the blending filament.

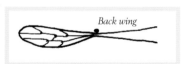

Back wing

Carefully cut out the wings, then stitch the thread tails through to the back. Insert both the wings through one hole at A, bend the wires under the applied wings and secure to the back with small stitches. Trim the wires.

7. Damselfly Abdomen

Following the instructions for Abdomen Method One (page 48), use one strand of bronze/black metallic thread (215c) in the size 12 Sharps needle (or beading needle), to work the abdomen with four bugle beads (72053) and two petite beads (42024). Use the same thread to work the fly stitch and 'tie-down'.

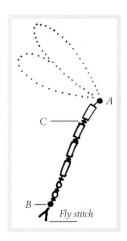

8. The Thorax

With nylon thread in the size 12 Sharps needle, apply a small piece of bronze snakeskin over the wire insertion point and the top of the abdomen to form the thorax (see Thorax Method Two, page 59).

9. The Head

Using nylon thread in the size 12 Sharps needle, apply a $1/8$" (3 mm) bead for the head, stitching with the hole towards the thorax, then apply a petite bead (40374) for the eye.

10. The Legs

Using two strands of bronze/black metallic cord in a size 9 Straw needle, work three (or six) legs with back stitches. Work a fly stitch for the antennae with a single strand of thread.

Snake skin

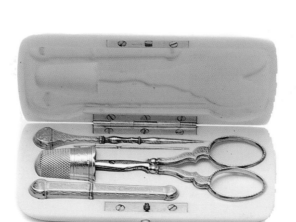

scendit (Inquit)in nauiculam,et trans
fretauit,et quid mirum.fratres. Chri
stus venit suscipere Infirmitates nostras,et
sua nobis conferre remedia sanitatis:quia
medicus qui non infert sanitatem,Infirmi
tates curare nescit,et qui non fuerit cum
infirmo.Infirmatus infirmo non potest
conferre sanitatem, Christus ergo et c

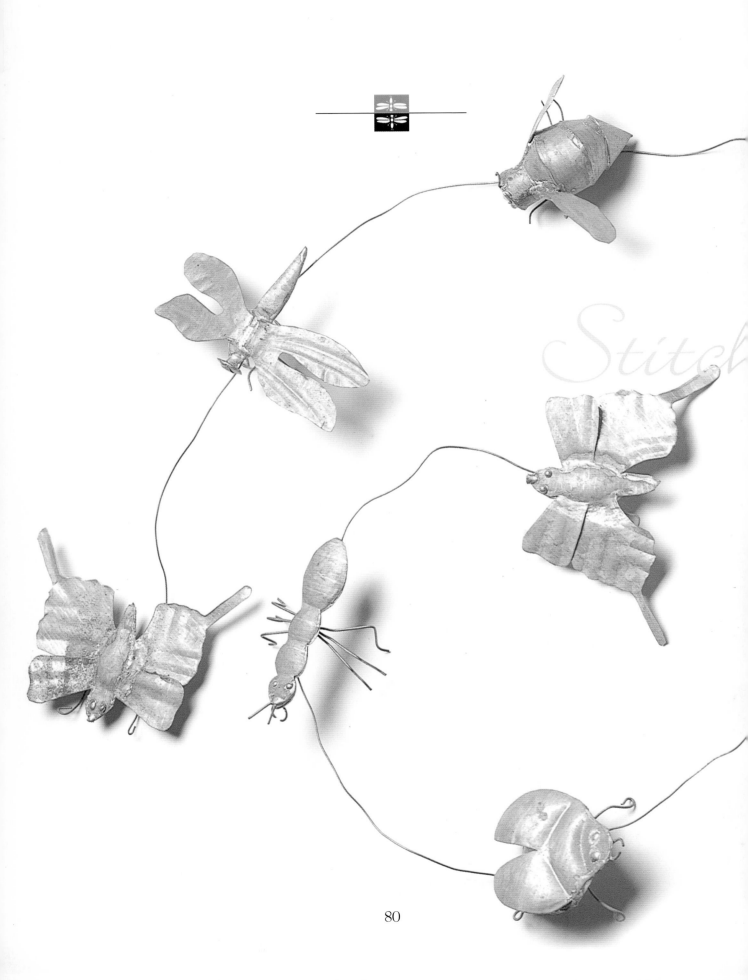

STITCH GLOSSARY

his glossary contains all the stitches used in this book and describes how the stitches have been worked for these projects. For ease of explanation, some of the stitches have been illustrated with the needle entering and leaving the fabric in the same movement. When working in a hoop this is difficult (or should be if your fabric is tight enough), so the stitches have to be worked with a stabbing motion, in several stages. The stitches are listed alphabetically for ease of reference.

Back Stitch

A useful stitch for outlining a shape. Bring the needle out at 1, insert at 2 (in the hole made by the preceding stitch) and out again at 3. Keep the stitches small and even.

Back Stitch – split

An easier version of split stitch, especially when using one strand of thread. Commence with a back stitch. Bring the needle out at 1, insert at 2 (splitting the preceding stitch) and out again at 3. This results in a fine, smooth line, ideal for stitching intricate curves.

Bullion Knots

These require some practice to work in a hoop. Use a Straw needle of the appropriate size, with the number of wraps depending on the length of the knot required. Bring the needle out at 1, insert at 2 leaving a long loop. Emerge at 1 again (not pulling the needle through yet) and wrap the thread around the needle the required number of times. Hold the wraps gently between the thumb and index finger of the left hand while pulling the needle through with the right hand. Pull quite firmly and insert again at 2, stroking the wraps into place.

Buttonhole stitch

These stitches can be worked close together or slightly apart. Working from left to right, bring the needle out on the line to be worked at 1 and insert at 2, holding the loop of thread with the left thumb. Bring the needle up on the line to be worked at 3 (directly below 2), over the thread loop and pull through to form a looped edge. If the stitch is shortened and worked close together over wire, it forms a secure edge for cut shapes, e.g. a detached leaf.

Buttonhole stitch – long and short

In long and short buttonhole stitch, each alternate stitch is shorter. Bring the needle out at 1, insert at 2 and up again at 3 (like an open detached chain stitch). When embroidering a petal, angle the stitches towards the centre of the flower.

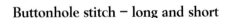

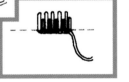

Detached buttonhole stitch

Buttonhole stitch can be worked as a detached filling, attached only to the background material at the edges of the shape. First work a row of back stitches around the shape to be filled. Change to a fine Tapestry needle. Bring the needle out at 1, work buttonhole stitches in to the top row of back stitches then insert the needle at 2. Come up again at 3 and work a buttonhole stitch into each loop of the preceding row. Insert the needle at 4. Quite different effects can be achieved when these stitches are worked close together or spaced apart.

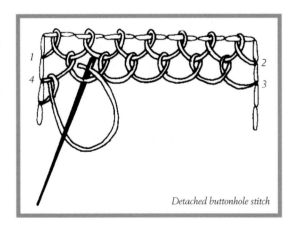

Detached buttonhole stitch

Corded detached buttonhole stitch

Detached buttonhole stitch can be worked over a laid thread. Outline the shape to be filled with back stitches. Using a Tapestry needle, come up at 1 and work the first row of buttonhole stitches into the top row of back stitches. Slip the needle under the back stitch at 2. Take the needle straight back to the left side and slip under the back stitch at 3. Work another row of

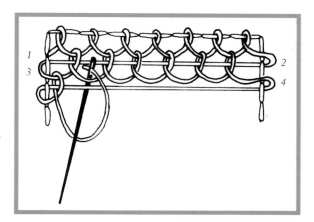

buttonhole stitches, this time taking the needle into the previous loops and under the straight thread at the same time. Slip the needle under the back stitch at 4 and continue as above.

To obtain a neater edge, the needle can be taken through to the back of the work at the end of each row (instead of under the back stitches), if preferred, e.g. the cornflower base. A contrasting thread (or gold thread), worked in another needle, can replace the straight thread, with interesting results.

Chain stitch

Bring the needle through at 1 and insert it again through the same hole, holding the loop of thread with the left thumb. Bring the needle up a short distance along at 2, through the loop, and pull the thread through. Insert the needle into the same hole at 2 (inside the loop) and make a second loop, hold, and come up at 3. Repeat to work a row of chain stitch, securing the final loop with a small straight stitch.

Chain stitch – whipped

This is a useful method for working slightly raised outlines. Work a row of chain stitch, then bring the needle out slightly to one side of the final securing stitch. Using either the eye of the needle or a Tapestry needle, whip the chain stitches by passing the needle under each chain loop from right to left, back to the beginning of the row. When whipped chain stitch is used for stems, the number of threads used can vary the thickness of the outline.

Couching

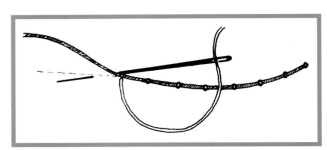

Couching, with tiny upright stitches worked at regular intervals, is a way of attaching a thread, or group of threads, to a background fabric. The laid thread is often thicker or more fragile (e.g. gold or chenille) than the one used for stitching. Couching stitches are also used for attaching wire to the base fabric before embroidering detached shapes.

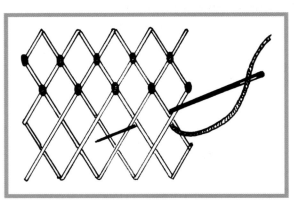

Couching – Lattice

Lattice couching is one of the endless variations of couched fillings. The design area is filled with a network of laid, parallel, evenly spaced threads. Where two threads cross, they are secured to the background with a small straight stitch.

Double running stitch

Double running stitch is identical on both sides of the fabric, and is most easily worked on even-weave cloth, where threads can be counted to produce even-length stitches.

1. First work a row of evenly spaced running stitches, by passing the needle through the fabric with an in-and-out movement, along the line to be covered.

2. Fill in the spaces left on the first journey with running stitches worked in the opposite direction (shown shaded in the diagram).

Feather stitch

This stitch is made up of a series of loops, stitched alternately to the right and to the left, each one holding the previous loop in place. Come up on the line to be followed at 1. Insert the needle to the right at 2 and come up on the line again at 3, holding the thread under the needle with the left thumb. Repeat on the left side of the line, reversing the needle direction, e.g. veins for the dragonfly.

Feather stitch – single

Work the feather stitch loops in one direction only. This stitch is very effective for working the veins in wings.

Fly stitch

Fly stitch is actually an open detached chain stitch. Bring the needle out at 1 and insert at 2, holding the working thread with the left thumb. Bring up again at 3 and pull through over the loop. Secure the loop with an anchoring stitch which can vary in length to produce different effects, e.g. a short tie-down stitch is used for antennae; a long tie-down stitch is taken through the beads when working the cerci at the end of a beaded dragonfly abdomen.

French knots

Using a Straw needle, bring the thread through at the desired place, wrap the thread once around the point of the needle and reinsert the needle. Tighten the thread and hold taut while pulling the needle through. To increase the size of the knot use more

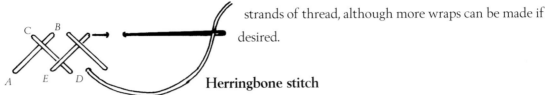

strands of thread, although more wraps can be made if desired.

Herringbone stitch

Herringbone stitch is a border stitch, worked from left to right, which is used to make a crossed, zigzag line. It can also be used to fill shapes, such as dragonfly's wings.

1. Bring the needle through the fabric on the lower line at A, then make a short stitch from right to left (B to C) a little further along the top line.
2. Make a second short stitch along the lower line (D to E), spacing the stitches evenly. Repeat along the row.

Long and short stitch

This stitch can be used to fill areas too large or irregular for satin stitch, or where shading is required. The first row, worked around the outline, consists of alternating long and short satin stitches. In the subsequent rows, the stitches are all of similar length, and fit into the spaces left by the preceding row. For a more realistic result when working petals, direct the stitches towards the centre of the flower. The surface will look smoother if the needle either pierces the stitches of the preceding row or enters at an angle between the stitches.

Overcast stitch

This stitch is made up of tiny, upright satin stitches, worked very close together over a laid thread or wire, resulting in a firm raised line. When worked over wire it gives a smooth, secure edge for cut shapes, e.g. dragonfly

Wire

86

wings. Place the wire along the line to be covered. Working from left to right with a stabbing motion, cover the wire with small straight stitches, pulling the thread firmly so that there are no loose stitches which may be snipped when the shape is cut out.

Pad stitch

Pad stitch is used as a foundation under satin stitch when a smooth, slightly raised surface is required. Padding stitches can be either straight stitches or chain stitches, worked in the opposite direction to the satin stitches. Felt can replace pad stitch for a more raised effect.

Wire

Pad stitch

Satin stitch

Satin stitch

Satin stitch is used to fill shapes. It consists of horizontal or vertical straight stitches, worked close enough together so that no fabric shows through, yet not overlapping each other. Satin stitch can be worked over a padding of felt or pad stitches and a smooth edge is easier to obtain if the shape is first outlined with split back stitch.

Stab stitch

Stab stitch is used to apply a leather or felt shape to the main fabric. It consists of small straight stitches made from the main fabric into the applied fabric, e.g. a thorax. Bring the needle out at 1 and insert at 2, catching in the edge of the applied piece.

Stem stitch

Worked from left to right, the stitches in stem stitch overlap each other to form a fine line suitable for outlines and stems. To start, bring the needle out at 1 on the line to be worked. Go down at

2, come up at 3 and pull the thread through. Insert the needle at 4, holding the thread underneath the line with the left thumb, and come up again at 2 (in the same hole made by the previous stitch) then pull the thread through. Go down at 5, hold the loop and come up again at 4, then pull the thread through. Repeat to work a narrow line.

Stem stitched band – raised

Stem stitch can be worked over a foundation of couched, padding thread to produce a raised, smooth, stem stitch band, ideal for insect bodies. Lay a preliminary foundation of padding stitches worked with soft cotton thread. Across this padding, at fairly regular intervals, work straight (couching) stitches at right angles to the padding thread

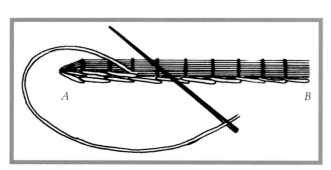

(do not make these stitches too tight). Then proceed to cover the padding by working rows of stem stitch over these straight stitches, using a Tapestry needle so as not to pierce the padding thread. All the rows of stem stitch are worked in the same direction, close together and ending either at the same point, e.g. A or spaced as in satin stitch, e.g. B.

Straight stitch

Individual straight stitches, of equal or varying length, can be stitched with a variety of threads to achieve interesting effects, e.g. insect legs in metallic thread.

Tacking (basting)

Tacking (or basting), a dressmaking term, is a row of running stitches – longer on the top of the fabric – used to temporarily mark an outline or to hold two pieces of fabric together.

Turkey knots

Turkey knots are worked then cut to produce a soft velvety pile, e.g. for cornflower heads. Although there are several ways to work Turkey knots, the following method works well for small areas. Use two strands of thread in a size 9 Crewel or Straw needle.

Insert the needle into the fabric at 1 and pull through, holding a 2″ (5 cm) tail with the left thumb. Come out at 2 and go down at 3 to make a small securing stitch. Bring the needle out again at 1 (can pierce the securing stitch), pull the thread down to form the second tail and hold with the left thumb.

For the second Turkey knot, insert the needle at 4, still holding the tail. Come out at 5 and go down at 2 to make a small securing stitch. Bring the needle out again at 4, pull the thread down and hold with the left thumb as before. Repeat to work a row.

Work each successive row directly above the previous row, holding all the resulting tails with the left thumb. To complete, cut all the loops, comb with an eyebrow comb, and cut the pile to the desired length. The more the pile is combed the fluffier it becomes.

Whipped spider web stitch

Whipped spider stitch is a form of needleweaving worked over a grid of foundation threads, which can be used to fill many different shapes, e.g. the poppy bud. First lay the foundation stitches, usually in a heavier thread, over the

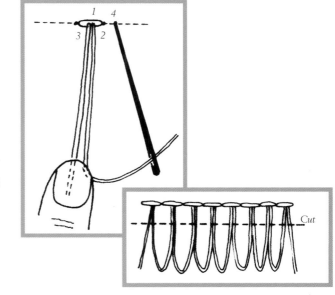

89

shape to be worked. Working from right to left, whip each of these laid threads with a back stitch, using a tapestry needle so as not to pierce the threads or the background fabric. Bring the needle out at the edge of the shape and slide under thread 1. Work a back stitch over 1 then slide the needle under thread 2. Work a back stitch over 2 then slide the needle under thread 3. Work a back stitch over 3 then insert the needle at the edge of the shape. Repeat, always working in the same direction, until the shape is filled, resulting in whipped 'ribs' on the surface.

To work a circular, raised, whipped spider web lay four long foundation stitches, as shown, securing the thread at the back of the work. Gather and tie all these threads together in the centre with a temporary length of thread. Using a tapestry needle, bring the working thread up between these threads and start whipping the spokes, working in a clockwise direction and pulling on the temporary thread at the same time, causing the web to be raised in the middle. Continue, working back over one strand and forward under two, until the spokes are filled to the required amount, then remove the spare thread, e.g. the centre of the Oriental poppy.

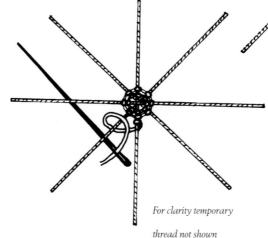

Temporary thread

For clarity temporary thread not shown

BIBLIOGRAPHY

Beck, Thomasina, *The Embroiderer's Garden*, David and Charles, London 1988.

Beck, Thomasina, *The Embroiderer's Flowers*, David and Charles, London, 1992.

Beck, Thomasina, *The Embroiderer's Story*, David and Charles, London, 1995.

Beck, Thomasina, *Gardening with Silk and Gold*, David and Charles, London, 1997.

Belk, Russell W, *Collecting in a Consumer Society*, Routledge, London, 1995.

Belk, Russell W, *On Collecting*, Routledge, London, 1995.

Christie, Grace, *Samplers and Stitches*, Batsford, London, 1920.

Dance, S. Peter, *The Art of Natural History*, Bracken Books, London, 1989.

Epstein, Diana & Safro, Millicent, *Buttons*, Thames and Hudson, London, 1991.

Floral Ornament, BookKing International, Paris, 1995.

Hughes, Therle n.d., *English Domestic Needlework 1660-1860*, Abbey Fine Arts, London.

Insects: An Illustrated Survey, Hamlyn, London, 1979.

King, Donald & Levey, Santina, *Embroidery in Britain from 1200 to 1750*, Victoria and Albert Museum, London, 1993.

Koch, Maryjo, *Dragonfly Beetle Butterfly Bee*, Smithmark, New York, 1998.

Mira Calligraphiae Monumenta c. 16th century, Facsimile copy, Thames and Hudson, London, 1992.

Naumann, I. D., *Systematic and Applied Entomology*, Melbourne University Press, 1994.

Nicholas, Jane, *Stumpwork Embroidery A Collection of Fruits, Flowers and Insects*, Milner, Sydney, 1995.

Nicholas, Jane, *Stumpwork Embroidery Designs and Projects*, Milner, Sydney, 1998.

Niwa, Motoji, *Japanese Traditional Patterns*, Vol. 1, Graphic-sha Publishing, Tokyo, 1990.

Nuridsany, Claude & Pérennou, Marie, *Microcosmos*, Stewart, Tabori and Chang, New York, 1996.

Snook, Barbara, *English Embroidery*, Bell and Hyman, London, 1974.

Swain, Margaret, *Historical Needlework*, Barrie and Jenkins, London, 1970.

Thomas, Mary, *Dictionary of Embroidery Stitches*, Hodder and Stoughton, London, 1935.

Urquhart, F. A., *Introducing the Insect*, F. Warne and Co., London, 1965.

Zahradnik, Jir, *The Illustrated Book of Insects*, Treasure Press, London, 1991.

Zborowski, Paul & Storey, Ross, *Field Guide to Insects in Australia*, Reed, Sydney, 1995.

ACKNOWLEDGEMENTS

I would like to extend my sincere thanks to all those fellow embroiderers who share my passion for insects – your gifts of information and insect specimens have bought great joy. My special thanks to Trudi Bean, for her initial idea of working a specimen box of stumpwork insects, also for sharing 'yet another insect book'.

I am indebted to The Winston Churchill Memorial Trust for granting me a Fellowship to study sixteenth and seventeenth century needlework in the United Kingdom in 1999. This was an inspirational journey for which I will be forever grateful.

To all those involved in the production of this book at Sally Milner Publishing – your expertise is greatly appreciated.

Finally, my special thanks to John, David, Katie and Joanna for their unfailing support and encouragement.

Stumpwork supplies *& kit information*

The threads and beads referred to in this book – Au Ver à Soie, Cifonda, DMC, Framecraft, Kreinik, Madeira, Mill Hill, Minnamurra, Needle Necessities – are available from specialist needlework shops.

A mail order service for embroidery and stumpwork supplies is available from JANE NICHOLAS EMBROIDERY. All materials required for the projects may be obtained either in kit form or individually. Please write or telephone for information and price list.

Jane Nicholas Embroidery

Chelsea Fabrics

277 Bong Bong Street

(PO Box 300)

Bowral New South Wales 2576

Australia

Tel/fax: 61 2 4861 1175

93

Jane Nicholas

Jane Nicholas is an experienced embroiderer in goldwork, crewel and ethnic embroidery but specialises in stumpwork. She has been researching this technique for more than sixteen years, during which time she has authored two books on the topic *Stumpwork Embroidery: A Collection of Fruits, Flowers and Insects for Contemporary Raised Embroidery* (1995) and *Stumpwork Embroidery: Designs and Projects* (1998). In 1999 Jane was awarded a Churchill Fellowship to pursue her passion and further her studies in the UK. Jane shares her skills and knowledge through regular classes in Australia and New Zealand and teaches for the Embroiderers' Guilds of the USA and Canada. Jane has a love of books and is an avid collector of old textiles, needlework tools and insect specimens – to embroider in stumpwork. She is married, has three children and lives in Bowral, New South Wales.

Books by the same author

Nicholas, Jane 1995, *Stumpwork Embroidery: A Collection of Fruits, Flowers and Insects for Contemporary Raised Embroidery*, Milner, Sydney.

Nicholas, Jane 1998, *Stumpwork Embroidery: Designs and Projects*, Milner, Sydney.

INDEX

ONE DIRECTION

POSTER ✿ COLLECTION

OVER 25 PULL-OUT POSTERS, PLUS: BONUS DOUBLE-SIZE POSTER

Global Merchandising Services

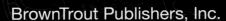

BrownTrout Publishers, Inc.

Photography by Simon Harris and John Urbano.

Published by BrownTrout Publishers, Inc.
201 Continental Blvd, Suite 200
El Segundo, CA 90245
Toll Free 800-777-7812
Outside US and Canada 310-607-9010

ISBN: 978-1-4650-1573-0

ONE DIRECTION
MORE 1D MERCH FOR YOUR WALLS!

YOU CAN NEVER GET ENOUGH OF **Zayn, Niall, Harry, Louis, and Liam,** so be sure to check out the Official 1D Wall Calendars, which come in 12" x 12" or mini 7" x 7" sizes!

And 1D comes to you larger than ever with our full-size, official 1D posters. There are a couple different ones to choose from and they're great to hang in your bedroom or special hangout spot.

Get your 1D calendars and posters today! They're available at most retailers.

Or call BrownTrout Publishers, Inc. at 800-777-7812 to find a retail location near you.

For other 1D merch, visit www.shop1D.com